Journey Between Worlds

A Memoir of Discovery, Identity, and Cross-Cultural Transformation

Betty Wakia

Papua New Guinea

Paperback ISBN: 978-1-7638456-9-5

First Published in 2026 by

First Nations Writers Festival International Limited T/as First Nations Publishers

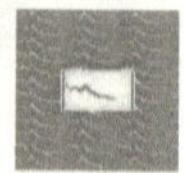

A Registered Charity (ABN 79 655 932 979)

2/53 Junction St, Nowra NSW 2540, Australia

Phone: +61 491 851 353

Email: firstnationswritersfestival@gmail.com
Web: www.firstnationswritersfestival.org
FB: www.facebook.com/firstnationswritersfestival.com

Cover Design: Busybird Publishing
Typeset: Busybird Publishing
Line Edited: Anna Borsi AM 2026
Printed and bound in Australia by IngramSpark

This is a Memoir. All place names and events are real and correct at the time of writing.

A catalogue record for this book is available from the National Library of Australia

To my parents,
Gabriel Guai Wakia and Maria Talime Wakia,
whose love, guidance, and unwavering
support have carried me across worlds
and made this journey possible.

Contents

ACKNOWLEDGMENTS

I would like to express my deepest gratitude to everyone who made this journey possible.

To my parents, for their unwavering love, encouragement, and guidance from my earliest days to this moment of sharing my story.

To my mentors and professors at Wuhan University of Technology and the Tianjin University of Technology and Education, whose wisdom and support shaped my academic path.

To my friends and colleagues across Papua New Guinea, China, and beyond, whose insights, laughter, and companionship made this journey richer and more meaningful.

Finally, to all the people I met along the way, in cities, villages, markets, and classrooms, who generously shared their culture, stories, and experiences — you are the heartbeat of this memoir.

1

THE DREAM
THAT WOULD NOT SLEEP

My earliest memories are of Koroba, nestled in the heart of Hela Province, where the mornings rise with mist rolling across the ridges like ancestral breath. The mountains stood tall as guardians, their slopes carved by streams that glittered under the sun, and the earth beneath my bare feet was cool, rich, and alive. To outsiders, our home might have seemed remote, untouched by the rush of the world. But to me, it was the centre of life, filled with voices, laughter, and stories that stitched together who we were.

My earliest memories are of the sound of voices. In the daytime, the voices of women carried across the gardens as they dug sweet potato, called to children, or laughed in conversation. The voices of men echoed through clan gatherings, debates and decisions. But in the evenings, when the fires were lit and the day's work was done, the voices that mattered most were those of the elders.

It was then that my grandfather would gather us close. He sat tall, even in his old age, with a presence that filled the room more than the firelight ever could. His face carried the lines of time, and his eyes seemed to hold the memory of generations. As the flames danced, he spoke. His voice was steady and strong, carrying stories older than books, older than schools, older than all the maps that outsiders carried into our land.

He told us who we were: the Huli people. He spoke of our clans, our land, and the ancestors who had walked before us. He reminded us that our strength came from the soil we gardened, the rivers that ran through our valleys, and the spirits that watched over us. He spoke of bilas—of the pride we wore in our feathers, wigs, and paint during ceremonies, but reminded us that true pride was not only in how we looked but in how we lived. His words were not merely stories for passing the night; they were instructions for living; seeds of wisdom planted in our hearts.

As a child, I sat in awe. I watched the shadows of the fire flicker on his face, and though I did not always understand every detail, I felt the weight of his words. In those moments, I belonged to something greater than myself. I belonged to my people, my land, and my history.

But even as I absorbed his teachings, my imagination stretched beyond the valleys. I often wondered what lay past the mountains that framed our world. When I ran across the gardens or chased after my cousins in the grass, I would stop and stare at the horizon, asking myself: What lies beyond those ridges? What kind of people live there? What languages do they speak?

Sometimes my grandfather's stories hinted at places far away—lands of traders, lands of ancient inventions, lands of power and mystery. One place, spoken of here and there, was China. To my child's mind, it sounded like a land from legend: a place of dragons, of great walls, of countless people. I had no map, no picture to hold, only a sense of vastness. The word itself seemed heavy, like it carried the weight of centuries.

At that age, the dream was not clear. I did not yet know what "studying abroad" meant. But the thought of stepping into worlds beyond Koroba stirred something restless inside me. Even as I laughed with cousins, fetched water with aunties, or sat quietly by the fire, there was always a small spark inside me that whispered: There is more beyond the valley.

Life in Koroba was full of joy in its own way. We lived close to the land. I remember running barefoot in the cool mud after the rain, the earth squelching between my toes. I remember the smell of smoke from cooking fires, the taste of freshly roasted kaukau, the feel of my mother's hands washing my hair. The days were woven with simple tasks, and yet they felt endless and full.

But when I was five years old, my world shifted. My father, who had been working in Port Moresby, wanted me to join him. Soon after, my mother and my little brother prepared to move with me.

The decision brought excitement and fear. For a small child who had known only the valleys and mountains, the idea of a city—of airplanes, of buildings, of so many strangers— was both thrilling and terrifying. I remember clinging to my mother's hand as we prepared to leave. My grandfather's eyes followed me that morning. He did not speak much, but when he placed his hand on my head, I felt his blessing settle over me like armour.

The journey itself is a blur of images: the descent from the cool highlands into the heavy heat of the lowlands, the strange sound of traffic roaring like angry rivers, the sight of buildings stacked close together, crowding the sky. My small body ached with the strangeness of it all. The city smelt of dust, petrol, and smoke, not of earth after rain.

In Port Moresby, life was unlike anything I had known. The days were louder, harsher, filled with movement. The safety of clan and valley was gone. Here, people spoke in many tongues, children played on dusty streets, and survival demanded a new kind of strength.

At first, I felt lost. I missed the voices of Koroba—the steady rhythm of my grandfather's wisdom, the laughter of cousins, the smell of gardens after morning rain. At night, I lay awake, wishing for the quiet comfort of the valleys. But slowly, I began to see that the city carried its own lessons. Schools introduced me to books and classrooms, to lessons about the wider world. The radio brought in news of distant places. People spoke of countries I could barely imagine, of opportunities that seemed far from my reach.

Yet, through it all, I carried my grandfather's voice with me. His stories lived inside me, reminding me who I was. They grounded me in moments when the city threatened to swallow me whole.

Looking back now, I see that the dream of studying abroad — of stepping into China — was born quietly in those years. It was planted by my grandfather's wisdom, watered by the challenges of city life, and nourished by my own curiosity. It was not loud, not yet. But it was there, a small flame that refused to go out.

No matter where I went, the dream followed me. It became the dream that would not sleep.

Port Moresby was a world away from Koroba, and to my five-year-old eyes, it felt like stepping on to another planet. The first thing I noticed was the heat. The cool highland air that kissed my skin in Koroba was replaced by a heavy blanket of humidity that clung to me. The sun felt closer, sharper. My little brother and I often sat sweating in the afternoon, our bodies longing for the crisp cool air of the mountains.

We lived with my father, who had been working in the city for some time before we joined him. His world was different from the one my grandfather had known. He woke early, dressed in shirts and trousers instead of the traditional wear of our people, and left for work each day with a seriousness I did not yet understand. At night, he often came home tired, his face lined with the weight of responsibility. But there was also pride in his eyes when he looked at me, as if he carried hope that I would grow into a different kind of life.

When my mother joined us with my little brother, our house became warmer. She carried Koroba with her in her cooking, her voice, her laughter. She planted a small garden even in the limited space of the city, as if to remind herself—and us—that we were still people of the soil. She told me often: "Never forget where you come from, even if you go far."

But the city pressed in on us. Port Moresby was crowded, restless, and sometimes dangerous. I remember walking with my mother to the market, clutching her hand tightly as we moved through the noise of vendors calling out, the smell of smoke, fried food, and dust rising from the ground. Unlike Koroba, where everyone knew each other, here people were strangers—faces that passed by without names, voices that carried in languages I did not understand.

School became the place where my world widened the most. At first, I was shy. The classrooms were filled with children from different provinces, each carrying their own accents, their own stories. Some laughed at the way I spoke, or the way I carried myself, as a girl who had come from the highlands. But my teachers encouraged me to keep learning. Slowly, I found my rhythm in reading, writing, and lessons that opened doors to new ideas.

It was in those classrooms that I first began to hear more about China. Teachers spoke of great inventions—paper, gunpowder, the compass—that had shaped the world. They spoke of a country that had risen from poverty to power, a nation of discipline and innovation. To me, the words sounded like something out of one of my grandfather's stories, except these tales were not about spirits or ancestors—they were about real people shaping the present.

Sometimes, when the teacher described the Great Wall, I closed my eyes and imagined myself standing on it, looking out over the vastness of a land so far from my own. It seemed impossible then, just as impossible as the moon above us seemed each night. But the dream took root.

At home, my parents encouraged me in their own way. My father, though strict, often told me, "Education is the road that can carry you further than the mountains." My mother, softer in her encouragement, always reminded me of the wisdom of my grandfather, urging me to hold on to my identity even as I reached for something new. Their words planted both ambition and responsibility in me.

Yet the city was not always kind. We faced struggles—money was often tight, and my parents sacrificed much to keep us in school. There were moments when I felt the weight of being different, of carrying not just my own dreams but also the hopes of my family and clan. I was reminded constantly that as a Huli woman; my path was not a common one. Many girls my age were expected to stay close to home, to marry young, to continue the cycle of life as it had always been.

But I could not quiet the dream. The seed planted in Koroba by my grandfather's stories, watered by the lessons of my parents, and nourished by the new world of Port Moresby, began to grow. It followed me everywhere—in the classroom, in the market, even in the quiet moments when I lay awake at night listening to the hum of the city.

I imagined myself boarding an airplane, crossing oceans, stepping onto foreign soil. I imagined learning in classrooms where the language was different, eating food I had never tasted, walking streets filled with faces I did not recognise. Sometimes, I imagined myself writing letters home, telling my family of the wonders I had seen. Other times, I imagined myself returning with knowledge, standing tall among my people, sharing what I had learned.

The dream was not only mine. It was tied to the voices of my family, my clan, my people. In every step I took, I carried

Koroba inside me—the valleys, the rivers, the wisdom of my grandfather. The dream to study abroad was not simply about leaving; it was about carrying my people with me into the wider world.

Even as a child, I sensed that the journey would not be easy. There would be struggles, sacrifices, and doubts. But the fire inside me refused to go out. It burned quietly but steadily, reminding me that one day, I would travel beyond Papua New Guinea. One day, I would see China with my own eyes.

And so, though I was still just a child navigating the streets of Port Moresby, the dream began to grow louder. It became the dream that would not sleep.

In Port Moresby, school became both a refuge and a battlefield. Every morning, I put on my uniform and walked into classrooms filled with the chatter of children from all over Papua New Guinea. Their stories were different from mine— some had grown up in the coast, some in the islands, others in the city itself. I was a child of the highlands, carrying the rhythm of the Huli language on my tongue and the memory of Koroba's valleys in my heart.

At first, I felt the difference like a stone in my shoe. Children teased me for my accent, for the way I stumbled over English words, for the shyness that came from being uprooted. Some laughed when I told them I was from Hela[1], as if the mountains were too far, too wild, to produce someone who could sit in a classroom with them. Their laughter stung, but it also strengthened something in me. I thought of my grandfather's voice around the fire, reminding me that we Huli carry pride not just in how we dress, but in how we live. His words echoed inside me: You know who you are. Stand tall.

––––––––––––––

1 - Hela Province, established in 2012 in Papua New Guinea's Highlands region, is a resource-rich area with a population of over 249,000. Known for the unique Huli Wigmen culture, the province is centered around the capital, Tari, and is economically driven by the $19 billion PNG LNG Project.

So, I learned to stand taller. I buried myself in my books, determined to master the lessons. Each word I learned in English felt like another stone placed in the bridge toward the world beyond. I listened carefully when teachers spoke of other countries, tracing their names with my pen as if writing them down would bring them closer.

The library at school became a kind of sacred place for me. I spent hours there, my fingers running across pages that carried me into worlds I could not yet see. One day, I found an old book about world history. It was there I first read, in more detail, about China—not just the Great Wall or dynasties, but about its people, its struggles, its strength in rebuilding itself into one of the most powerful nations of the modern world. I remember staring at a black-and-white photograph of Beijing, the streets crowded with bicycles, and thinking: one day, I will walk there.

At home, my father pushed me harder than anyone else. He did not praise easily; instead, he demanded results. His words were often strict, sometimes sharp, but beneath them I felt his hope for me. He wanted me to succeed, to walk a road he could not walk himself. My mother, on the other hand, was my comfort. She reminded me to stay true to myself, to hold onto the values of respect, humility, and resilience. Between the two of them, I learned balance—ambition from my father, grounding from my mother.

Life in Port Moresby was never without struggle. Some days we had little money. Sometimes the city's dangers brushed close to us—fight on the streets, theft, the constant warning to be careful after dark. There were moments I longed desperately for Koroba, for the safety of clan and kin, where every face was familiar. Yet those struggles in the city toughened me. They taught me that to survive in a world much larger than my village, I would need not only knowledge, but also resilience and courage.

As I grew older, the dream inside me became clearer. At first, it had been only a whisper, a restless curiosity. But now, it had taken shape: I wanted to study abroad. I wanted to go to China. I wanted to see with my own eyes the places I had only read about in books and heard about in classrooms.

The thought both thrilled and frightened me. Who was I, a girl from Hela, to think I could walk in the streets of Beijing or Shanghai? Who was I to dream of standing on the Great Wall, of learning in classrooms where the language was strange and the expectations higher than anything I had known? Many times I questioned myself. But each time doubt rose, the dream pushed back. It refused to be silenced.

Sometimes, late at night, I lay awake listening to the hum of the city. I imagined an airplane roaring overhead, its lights cutting across the sky. I wondered where it was going—Singapore, Hong Kong, perhaps even Beijing. I imagined myself inside, looking out of the window as the lights of Port Moresby faded beneath me, carrying me toward a new horizon.

In those quiet moments, I understood something deeply: the dream was no longer just mine. It was tied to my family, to the sacrifices my parents had made, to the blessings of my grandfather, to the identity of being Huli. If I succeeded, I would not walk alone—I would carry my people with me. I would carry the valleys of Koroba, the voices of my ancestors, the pride of the highlands.

The dream had been planted in me as a child in Koroba, nurtured in the challenges of Port Moresby, and now it had grown into something I could not ignore. It became a fire that lit every step I took, every lesson I learned, every prayer I whispered.

It was, truly, the dream that would not sleep.

2

MY CHILDHOOD
IN PORT MORESBY

In 1992, I was five years old when I left Koroba for Port Moresby to be with my father. That was the year my childhood took a new turn, a year when the red earth of the Highlands gave way to the humid air of the city, and my small world stretched beyond the misty ridges of my homeland. I can still feel the weight of that journey, even now, as if it were stitched into the lining of my memory. My mother's tears were on my skin as she hugged me goodbye, her voice urging me to listen to my father and be a good girl. I was only a child, but I knew that leaving Koroba meant leaving behind more than the mountains. I was stepping into my father's world, the world of books, politics, and city life.

My father was working with the Department of Foreign Affairs and Trade at Waigani at that time. His job was a big one, though I could not fully understand it as a child. All I knew was that when people in the village spoke of him, their voices carried both respect and curiosity. "He works with the government," they would say, and those words sounded heavy, like something you could not touch but could only admire from afar. To me, he was not just a man in an office. He was my father, a bookworm, a dreamer, a man who had walked barefoot from Koroba to Tari just to reach school, carrying hunger and determination like two companions by his side.

He loved books so much that the house in Port Moresby was filled with them. Boxes of novels and comics, stacks of newspapers, journals that smelled of ink and dust. Among all those, one treasure bound us together most: The Phantom. My father and I were obsessed with those comics. We would fight over who would read them first. Sometimes I would wake early, before the sun rose over Boroko, and sneak into the boxes to pull one out. I would read quickly, trying to finish before he noticed. But somehow, he always knew. "You read it before me, eh?" he would tease, his eyes twinkling behind his glasses. We would laugh and wrestle over the next one, and I felt proud that he treated me as an equal in that little world of imagination.

The Phantom was more than just a story to us. To me, he was a hero in purple, walking through jungles, standing against injustice, a man of courage and mystery. To my father, he was a mirror of resilience, someone who kept fighting no matter how many times the world turned against him. Maybe, in some way, the Phantom reflected my father's own struggles.

But my father gave me more than books. He gave me knowledge that in our Huli culture was usually reserved for men. The first lessons he taught me were about his clan, our tribes, and our genealogy. Normally, these stories, the long recitations of names and bloodlines, belonged to the men's house. Women were not supposed to hear them in such detail. Yet my father broke that barrier. He said to me, "You must know where you come from. You must carry this knowledge because one day, women will stand equal in this country, and you will need it."

I was too young to understand the weight of his words, but I carried them like treasures. While other girls my age played with dolls or jumped rope, I sat by my father's side, listening as he traced the roots of our people, naming ancestors who lived before the time of white men, recounting wars, alliances, and the meaning of each clan name. His voice was like a drum, steady, repetitive, full of rhythm. I would memorise, repeat, and hold the stories in my heart, knowing I was being given something sacred.

Politics was another inheritance from him. My father lived and breathed politics. It filled the house the way the smell of kaukau fills the kitchen. At dinner, he spoke of Members of Parliament, their portfolios, their alliances, their betrayals. In the mornings, as he tied his tie and prepared for work, he spoke of new policies, international relations, debates in Parliament. Even in the evenings, when he was tired, lying on his bed with a book in his hand, his voice would wander back to politics. "These 109 members, they shape our future," he would say, and he made me memorise their names, their roles, their ministries. I could recite them like a song. Sometimes I wondered if he ever stopped thinking of politics. Once I joked, "Papa, the only place you don't talk politics is in the toilet." He laughed until his stomach shook and said, "True, my daughter, true."

He sacrificed much for my education. From his little, hard-earned salary, he enrolled me at Korobosea International School because he believed in quality education. He knew what it meant to struggle without it. His own childhood was marked by the absence of privilege. He grew up in a polygamous household where his father's love was stretched thin across many wives and many children. He often told us the story of how he would walk barefoot from Koroba to Tari Secondary School, carrying only determination in his pocket. Sometimes, when I saw him counting coins carefully at the table, or when he skipped buying new clothes so that I could have new textbooks, I could almost feel his pain—the pain of a man determined to give his children the opportunities he never had.

In Port Moresby, life was so different from Koroba. The city smelled of diesel and dust, not of fresh earth and sweet potatoes. The noise was constant—cars, shouting, radios, music spilling from houses. I missed the mountains, the mist that covered the mornings, the sound of pigs grunting outside the house. But I also felt something exciting about the city. It was a place of movement, of possibilities. My father told me, "This city is the heart of Papua New Guinea. From here, you can see the whole country."

At five years old, I did not understand the whole country, but I understood that my father's love and vision were shaping me. He was not just raising a daughter; he was preparing me for something larger.

At Korobosea International School, I stepped into a world that felt far away from the Highlands. The children I met there came from all over—some from Australia, some from Europe, some from the coastal provinces of PNG. Their skins were different colours, their accents carried strange sounds, and their lunches smelled of food I had never tasted before. I was a shy little Huli girl, standing in my second-hand uniform, clutching the strap of my school bag like a shield.

My father had walked me to class on the first day. I remember his hand, rough and warm, holding mine tightly as we entered the compound. His confidence was like a cloak around me. He told me, "Don't be afraid. Education is the bridge. Once you cross it, you can stand equal with anyone in the world." His words sank into me, though I did not fully understand them.

The classrooms were bright, with posters of animals, alphabets, and maps covering the walls. I loved staring at the world map, my finger tracing places I could barely pronounce: Brazil, Canada, India. My imagination travelled faster than my understanding. But even then, I knew that the world was vast, and one day, I wanted to see it beyond the dusty streets of Port Moresby.

School was not always easy. English was still new to me, and though I could speak Tok Pisin and Huli, I sometimes stumbled in class. There were times when other children laughed at my accent, or when I mispronounced a word, my cheeks burned with shame. But every evening, my father would sit with me, correcting my reading, helping me with spelling, making me read out loud from the Phantom comics or from old textbooks he had collected. He would clap his hands and say, "See, my daughter, you are improving. One day you will read faster than me."

The library became my secret kingdom. I discovered Nancy Drew, Hardy Boys, and storybooks from Australia that spoke of beaches, farms, and snow. Snow! I could not even imagine it properly. I would press my cheek against the book's pages, trying to picture how it would feel to hold ice in my hands, to see white covering the ground. My father laughed when I told him, "Papa, one day I will see snow." He replied, "Then you must study hard. Books will take you there before your feet do."

Life in Port Moresby was also dangerous. I remember the blackouts that swept through the city without warning. The lights would vanish, and the house would sink into darkness. Outside, we could hear shouting, dogs barking, sometimes gunshots in the distance. My father would light a kerosene lamp and tell us not to be afraid. "The city is restless," he would say, "but inside this house, you are safe." Still, my heart would pound, and I missed the quiet safety of Koroba, where the only night sounds were insects and owls.

One memory stays sharp within me. One evening, thieves tried to break into our neighbour's house. I woke to the sound of metal crashing, people shouting. My father got up, his face tight, and told us children to stay in the bedroom. He went outside with other men from the compound, carrying nothing but a stick in his hand. I remember pressing my face against the window, my breath fogging the glass, as I saw shadows moving in the darkness. Later, he returned, sweaty and angry, muttering about lawlessness and failed leadership. That night, I realised how fragile life in the city was, how much courage it took to live there.

At school, I began to make friends. One was a girl from Manus whose laughter was like a bell. She taught me to play elastics with a long band, jumping in rhythm until we were both breathless. Another was a boy from Australia who showed me his Game Boy. I watched in awe as tiny figures moved across the screen. I did not own such toys, but I never felt jealous. Instead, I felt curious. I wanted to know the world, to understand why some children had so much and others so little.

My father's political conversations fed this curiosity. At dinner, as we ate rice and tinned fish or kaukau boiled soft, he would speak of inequality, corruption, and leadership. Sometimes his words went over my head, but I listened closely. He would slam his hand on the table, his voice rising. "These leaders must serve the people! They forget where they come from." I watched his passion, the way his eyes blazed. I thought to myself, I want to have that fire too.

But not all of childhood was serious. I remember the games in the compound with other children—chasing each other until dusk, playing hide-and-seek behind the hibiscus bushes, climbing guava trees and eating the fruit with sticky fingers. When I laughed, when the sweat ran down my back and the air was filled with our voices, I felt free. For a while, the weight of expectations, of being the daughter of a man who carried so much, slipped away.

Yet even in play, the Highlands girl in me never left. When the other girls played with Barbie dolls, I found myself making small dolls out of cloth scraps, like we did back home. When they spoke of cartoons, I spoke of the mountains, of pigs, of gardens where food grew with the rain. They looked at me strangely sometimes, but I held onto my roots. My father always told me, "Never forget Koroba. You may live in the city, but your blood belongs to the mountains."

And so, I carried Koroba inside me, even as Port Moresby became my new home.

Every morning in Port Moresby began with my father's footsteps. I would hear him rise before the sun, the sound of the kettle whistling, the smell of instant coffee drifting through the house. He had a ritual that I came to know by heart: iron his shirt until it was crisp, polish his shoes until they shone, carefully knot his tie. I would watch from the doorway, still half-asleep, as he transformed from the man I knew at home into the man who stepped into government offices. He looked taller when he was dressed for work, his shoulders squared, his face serious.

Before he left, he would always check on me. "School today, eh?" he would say, his voice gentle, though his eyes carried the weight of responsibility. He would press a coin on my right palm, then walk out with his black briefcase swinging at his side. That briefcase fascinated me. It was like a treasure chest of papers, pens, and secrets. Sometimes, when he wasn't looking, I would peek inside, pulling out a document or two. I couldn't understand the big words, but I loved the feel of the papers, the smell of ink and government. It felt like touching the veins of the country itself.

My mornings after he left were filled with the rush of school. My uniform always felt too stiff, my shoes sometimes too tight, but I wore them with pride. At Korobosea International School,

I began to find my place, though it took time. I remember one teacher, a tall Australian woman with short blonde hair, who always smiled at me when I answered questions. She had a way of encouraging me without saying much, just a nod or a small clap. Her kindness gave me confidence, especially when my English faltered. Slowly, I found myself raising my hand more often, even if my voice shook.

School lunches were another kind of education. Other children brought sandwiches, fruit, juice boxes. My lunch was usually rice with tinned fish, sometimes a boiled sweet potato wrapped in foil. At first, I felt shy opening my container, worried the smell would make others laugh. But then one girl, curious, asked to taste my kaukau. She loved it, and soon I realised that food was not something to be ashamed of—it was a story, a gift from home.

There were moments, of course, when I longed for Koroba. The city never smelled of earth after rain. There were no pigs wandering freely, no gardens to weed, no women calling to each other across the ridges. In the compound, we were surrounded by fences and locks, always cautious of danger outside. I missed the openness of the village, the way we belonged to each other. In Port Moresby, people lived behind walls, suspicious of neighbours, afraid of *raskols*. Even as a child, I could feel the difference between the Highlands community and the city's distance.

But my father worked hard to bridge that gap for me. On weekends, he would take me to Ela Beach. I remember the heat of the sand under my feet, the salty smell of the sea, the sight of people swimming and laughing. Sometimes we bought ice blocks—sweet, cold relief in the burning sun. He would tell me stories as we walked along the shore: about his childhood walks to Tari, about the dreams he carried for me, about the kind of Papua New Guinea he wanted to see in the future. The ocean stretched before us like a possibility itself, endless and wide.

At night, after dinner, our house became a classroom again. My father would sit with his books, and I would sit with mine. He had a way of turning learning into adventure. When we read The Phantom, he would pause and ask, "What do you think makes him brave?" I would answer in my childish way, but slowly, I began to see that he was teaching me to question, to analyse, to find meaning beyond the story.

Politics, of course, was always present. He taught me the names of the 109 members of Parliament as if they were characters in another comic series. I memorised them like a song, repeating them until I knew each portfolio by heart. Sometimes, when guests came over, he would make me recite them. Their eyes would widen in surprise. "This little girl knows more politics than us!" they would laugh. I felt proud, but also a little burdened. I was only a child, yet already carrying the weight of a political education.

One day, after listening to him rant about corruption and failed policies, I asked, "Papa, why do leaders forget the people?" He looked at me for a long time, then said softly, "Because power is heavy, and some men cannot carry it with honour. That is why you must study, my daughter. One day, you will carry it better." His words planted a seed in me, though it would take years to grow.

The city also taught me about inequality in ways that no classroom could. I saw children selling *buai* on the streets, barefoot, their eyes hungry. I saw beggars sitting outside shops, their hands stretched out. I saw shiny cars pass by, filled with people who never looked out their windows. Even at my young age, I felt the sting of injustice. I thought of my father's sacrifices, his careful counting of coins, his stories of walking barefoot. I understood, in a way that pierced my heart, that life was not fair. But instead of despair, I felt determination. If my father could rise from nothing, barefoot on the road to Tari, then maybe I too could climb higher than the fences around us.

At school, I worked hard. Exams became small battles I wanted to win, not just for myself, but for my father. When I brought home good grades, he would beam with pride. Sometimes he would lift me high into the air, spinning me around, laughing. "See? You are smarter than me already!" he would say. His joy made all the late-night studying worth it.

Still, there were lonely days. I missed my mother's cooking, her voice calling me in the garden. I missed my cousins, the laughter of the village. Sometimes, lying in bed at night, I would cry quietly, pressing my face into the pillow so my father would not hear. But in the mornings, I woke up stronger. I reminded myself of his words: education is the bridge. And so, I kept walking across that bridge, one step at a time.

Looking back now, I see how those years in Port Moresby shaped me. They taught me resilience, curiosity, and the value of sacrifice. They gave me the fire of my father's politics, the love of books, the courage to dream beyond the boundaries of Koroba. But they also rooted me in my Huli identity, reminding me never to forget where I came from.

I was only five when I arrived in Port Moresby, a small girl with wide eyes and nervous steps. But by the time I left, I carried in me the seeds of who I would become—a woman shaped by two worlds, grounded in the mountains yet reaching toward the ocean, holding my father's dreams in one hand and my own in the other.

And so, my childhood in Port Moresby was not just a chapter of growing up. It was the beginning of a journey, a crossing from the safe ridges of childhood into the restless heart of a city, and into the lessons that would follow me all my life.

3

MY JOURNEY BEGINS

Life at UPNG settled into its familiar rhythm — lectures during the day, study sessions deep into the night, and hotel shifts to cover my living expenses. Yet beneath the surface of that routine, I carried the weight of a dream I could

not let go. I remembered the countless envelopes I had sealed over the years, each one heavy with my hopes, prayers, and determination, only to return to me with rejection stamped in silence.

Then, one hot afternoon, as I walked back from campus under the unforgiving Port Moresby sun, my phone rang. I nearly ignored it, but something urged me to answer. The voice on the other end was firm yet kind: *"Congratulations. You have been selected as one of eighteen students from Papua New Guinea to receive the Chinese Government Scholarship for 2011."*

The words struck me like lightning. I froze, unable to breathe, then asked him to repeat it. When he did, my knees weakened, and tears filled my eyes. Years of struggle, doubt, and whispered prayers collapsed into that single moment. I thought of the six rejections that had nearly broken me, the friends who mocked me, the nights when hope dimmed, and the parents who had never stopped believing.

When I shared the news, my mother wept with joy, raising her voice in thanksgiving. My father, ever a man of few words, simply said, *"You did not give up, and now you see the reward."* My siblings danced and cheered, and soon neighbours filled our home with food, laughter, and celebration. The scholarship did not feel like mine alone—it belonged to all of us.

Yet beneath the joy lay a deeper weight. This opportunity was more than a personal victory. I carried with me the hopes of my family, my clan, my province, and my country. I was going to China not only to study but to represent.

The weeks before departure were filled with farewells and blessings. Relatives came with advice, with food, with tears. My mother packed small reminders of home into my bag: a bilum she had woven, kaukau carefully wrapped, a shell necklace to wear close to my heart. My father gave me words that became a compass in my soul: "Respect the people you meet. Learn their ways, but never forget where you come from."

The day of departure finally arrived. At Jacksons International Airport, my family clung to me as though they could hold time still. My mother's trembling hands refused to let go, my father's steady nod carried unspoken pride, and my siblings laughed nervously, half in disbelief that I was truly leaving. When the boarding call came, I hugged them one last time, inhaled the familiar scent of home, and walked toward the gate without looking back.

From the window of the plane, as Port Moresby's green hills and blue waters disappeared beneath the clouds, I pressed my forehead against the glass and whispered a promise: *"I will make the most of this chance. I will not waste it."* In that moment, the voice of the Huli woman within me answered: *"Go, child. The land of your ancestors walks with you. The soil of Hela clings to your feet. The world will know who you are."*

That voice carried me back to where it all began.

Growing up in Papua New Guinea, the thought of studying in China seemed distant, almost unreachable. Yet dreams have a way of whispering across the years, refusing to fade. For us, education was more than personal ambition—it was a bridge to the future, a lifeline for families, tribes, and whole communities. My father, who never had the chance to study further, often reminded me, *"Books will take you to places where our feet cannot walk."* My mother added her wisdom: *"Knowledge is the garden no one can burn down."*

I grew up on stories told by firelight—stories of sacrifice and perseverance. Mothers selling produce in the markets, fathers hauling coffee bags across rough terrain, siblings sharing clothes so one could afford school fees. From those stories, I learned that any chance at education must be grasped firmly, not only for oneself but for all who believed in you.

At UPNG, where I studied Political Science and Law while working shifts at Airways Hotel, I learned the discipline of balance. The exhaustion of juggling lectures, late-night study, and long hours behind the hotel counter shaped me into someone resilient, someone who could endure. It was there that I first heard about the Chinese Government Scholarship—a golden opportunity to study in one of the fastest-growing nations in the world, a place where ancient culture met modern transformation.

The application process, however, tested more than my academic readiness. In those days, nothing was online. Every form had to be collected, completed by hand, photocopied, and submitted with a mountain of supporting documents—birth certificates, references, medical clearances. Each attempt required time, money, and patience.

My first application was rejected. I told myself it was fine—I would try again. The second rejection followed. Then the third. The fourth. The fifth. By the sixth rejection, hope nearly crumbled. Friends teased me, some mocking openly, others gently advising me to stop wasting my time. "Maybe this dream is not yours," they said. For a while, I almost believed them.

But I remembered Thomas Edison, who failed thousands of times before inventing the light bulb. If he had given up at six failures, the world might have waited much longer for light. His story sparked something in me again. If Edison could keep going, who was I to surrender so easily?

Another voice rose within me—the ancient voice of the Huli woman. She spoke with the strength of the highlands: *"We, Huli women, are not strangers to struggle. Do you think kaukau grows without sweat? Do you think firewood gathers itself? Failure is soil. Soil buries, but soil also nourishes. From it, new life can grow."*

I thought of the Huli women I had known since childhood—carrying bilums heavy with kaukau, firewood, and babies, walking long distances with quiet strength. They did not quit because their families depended on them. Their resilience flowed into me, and I knew I could not stop.

So I tried again. For the seventh time, I gathered my documents, sealed the envelope, and whispered to myself: *"This is my light bulb attempt number one thousand and one."* Unlike the earlier applications, this one carried no desperation—only calm resolve.

And when the call finally came, everything changed. The door that had been shut so many times opened at last. My path of rejection had become a story of perseverance. My struggle had turned into triumph. And my journey—to China, and far beyond—had truly begun.

4

FIRST IMPRESSIONS OF CHINA

The roar of the airplane engines that August morning in 2011 was more than just a sound—it was a signal that my life was about to change forever. As the aircraft lifted into the sky from Jackson's International Airport, I felt a strange mix of emotions swirling inside me: excitement, nervousness, pride, and a lingering sadness at leaving my family behind. I pressed my face to the cold window and watched as Port Moresby grew smaller and smaller, the familiar green hills and blue waters fading into the distance. I whispered a silent goodbye to my homeland, promising myself I would return with stories, knowledge, and achievements that would make them proud.

This was my first time leaving Papua New Guinea. Until then, the world beyond my island nation had existed only through textbooks, magazines, and flickering images on television. Now, I was not only stepping into that wider world but doing so as one of eighteen students chosen from thousands of applicants across the country.

The honour carried a heavy weight, but in that moment, as clouds stretched endlessly beneath us, it felt like wings had been given to my dream. I thought of my home in Hela Province, the rugged mountains, the valleys echoing with the chants of *singsings*, the smell of earth after the rain.

In my mind's eye, I could see my mother's hands busy preparing kaukau in the mumu, hear the low murmur of elders talking by the fire, feel the cold mist that clung to the early mornings of Koroba. Those images clung to me as I sat in my seat, miles above the ground, as though they were reminders of where I had come from and why I was on this journey.

Yet alongside the comfort of memory was an undercurrent of fear. I had never been on such a long journey before. The idea of travelling across oceans, of setting foot in countries whose names felt foreign in my mouth, was overwhelming. Would I be able to survive? Would I manage in a place where I did not know the language, where the food, the climate, even the rhythm of life itself, would be so different from everything I knew? These questions buzzed in my head like restless insects.

I remembered the moment my name had been announced as one of the scholarship recipients. My family and clan had celebrated with pride. They dressed me in my bilas, my face painted in the colours of our tribe, and they told me I was not going just for myself, but for them—for Hela, for Papua New Guinea. The burden of their hopes weighed heavily on me now, high above the Pacific Ocean. It was a sweet burden, but a burden nonetheless.

I leaned back in my seat and closed my eyes, listening to the steady thrum of the engines. To others, it might have been just background noise, but to me, it was the heartbeat of destiny, carrying me toward a life that until then had felt like a distant dream. I thought of all the sacrifices my parents had made, the nights they had gone without so I could have books, the mornings they had walked miles to find ways to pay for my education. Each vibration of the engine seemed to echo their voices: *Make this journey worthwhile. Do not forget where you come from.*

As the flight attendants moved through the aisle, serving meals and drinks, I looked at my fellow students. Some chatted nervously, others stared quietly out the windows, lost in their own thoughts. We were all so young, carrying with us the weight of our families and provinces, stepping into the unknown. In that moment, I realised we were not just individuals—we were representatives of our country. That thought gave me strength.

The further the plane travelled, the further I felt myself being stretched between two worlds—the world I had known all my life, and the world that awaited me. My heart beat with both fear and anticipation, but I reminded myself of something my grandfather had once told me: *"A bird does not learn to fly by staying in the nest. It must leap, and only then will its wings be tested."*

This journey was my leap. And though I did not yet know where it would take me, I resolved to face it with courage.

When the plane touched down in Singapore, I pressed my face against the window, my eyes wide like a child seeing the world for the first time. The lights of the runway glittered in neat lines, like strings of pearls laid carefully across the darkness. I had never seen a city so bright, so orderly, so full of movement, even in the middle of the night. As a Huli woman from the green valleys of Hela Province, where the mountains rise like guardians and the mist clings to the earth each morning, this view felt like another universe.

When we stepped off the plane, the air struck me first—it was thick, heavy with humidity, but it carried a scent I could not describe, a mixture of flowers, fuel, and the faint saltiness of the sea. The airport itself felt like a vast city under one roof. Changi International Airport glowed with polished floors and shining glass, so clean and organised that I almost hesitated to walk on it, as though I might leave muddy footprints from my highlands home.

I clutched my small bag tightly, holding it close to my chest as I followed the stream of passengers through the bright corridors. The signs above us flashed in English, Chinese,

Malay, and Tamil, reminding me that this was not one place but many, woven together. For a moment, I felt small and lost, like a single leaf swept into a mighty river. Yet inside me, there was also wonder.

I had four hours to wait before my connecting flight to Beijing, and as I walked through the terminal, I realised this airport was not like the ones I had known before.

Jackson's Airport in Port Moresby had been a place of dust, of crowded lines, of family members calling out their goodbyes with tears in their eyes. Here, there were fountains that danced, shops that gleamed with gold jewelry and glittering watches, and travellers who strolled casually, as though walking through a grand marketplace.

The bathrooms, of all things, amazed me. They smelled of flowers, and the water flowed at the wave of a hand. I laughed to myself, thinking of the pit latrines back home in Hela, or even the simple flush toilets in Port Moresby. Here, even the smallest details spoke of a world that valued order, comfort, and beauty.

I wandered further, my eyes drinking in everything. There were gardens inside the airport itself—green corners filled with orchids in colours so bright they looked unreal. I touched the petals softly, wondering if they were made of silk, but they were alive, breathing, their fragrance faint but sweet. I remembered the gardens of Hela, where wild orchids cling to tree trunks, their beauty uncelebrated except by those who pause to notice them. In this airport, those flowers were celebrated, displayed like treasures.

I stopped at a large glass window overlooking the runway. Beyond it, planes of every size and shape moved in silence, their lights blinking as they carried people to places I could hardly imagine. I pressed my hand to the glass, and for the first time in my life, I felt the true vastness of the world. Papua New Guinea, with all its beauty and struggles, was just one small island among so many. That thought did not make me feel insignificant; rather, it filled me with a strange fire, as though I had stepped into the beginning of a much greater journey.

I had some money in my pocket, exchanged from PNG kina into Singapore dollars, and I decided to try something new. I walked into a food court where the air was filled with aromas that made my stomach rumble. There were dishes lined up behind glass—noodles, rice, seafood, curries—and I could not even name most of them. The stall attendants smiled at me, speaking in English that was fast but clear. I pointed at a bowl of noodles with roasted duck, and when I took my first bite, I nearly cried. The richness of the broth, the softness of the noodles, the savory meat—it was so different from kaukau, taro, or pit-cooked pork, yet it filled me with the same sense of satisfaction. I thought of my mother, who would have laughed at me struggling with chopsticks, but I managed, slowly, one slippery noodle at a time.

As I ate, I watched people around me. Businessmen in suits tapped on laptops, families shepherded children with sleepy eyes, and young couples leaned close together, laughing softly. Each of them was heading somewhere, carrying stories I would never know. I felt like I was sitting at the crossroads of the world.

After my meal, I walked again, this time through the shops that seemed more like museums. Watches ticked behind glass cases, perfumes sparkled in tall bottles, and clothes hung with prices that made my heart stop. I did not buy anything, but I admired them as one admires stars—beautiful, distant, and unreachable. Yet even as I looked, I reminded myself that knowledge, not luxury, was my treasure. I was not in this place to shop, but to learn, to carry something far more lasting back to my people.

I paused again at the gardens, where butterflies floated lazily in the warm air. For a moment, I forgot I was in an airport at all.

I closed my eyes and thought of Hela, of the crisp morning air, the sight of men in bilas at a *singsing*, the sound of pigs grunting in the village yard. I felt the ache of homesickness tug at me, but also the thrill of adventure pushing me forward.

I had thought that four hours would feel long, but in Singapore it slipped through my fingers like water. There was too much to see, too much to marvel at, and I found myself walking faster, as though I could somehow gather the entire airport into my memory before it was time to leave.

I passed through a section filled with art displays, and I stopped at one that looked like a sculpture of metal birds rising into the air. They seemed to float, caught in mid-flight, and for a long while I stood staring at them. In Hela, I had grown up watching the flight of real birds—parrots with their bright green feathers, cockatoos flashing white against the jungle canopy, and the rare bird of paradise, dancing with its golden plumes in the morning sun. Those birds belonged to our myths and our songs; they carried messages from the spirit world, reminding us of the sacredness of our land. These metal birds in Singapore were different, yet they spoke to me in another way. They seemed to say: the human spirit also longs to fly, to break the boundaries of land and distance, to move freely across the sky.

I thought then of my ancestors, who never travelled beyond the mountains of Hela, whose world was marked by rivers, ridges, and valleys. Would they believe that I, their granddaughter, stood now in an airport surrounded by people from every corner of the globe, about to board a plane that would carry me to China? Would they understand this journey, or would they shake their heads in disbelief?

Perhaps both. But I felt them with me. I carried their strength, their courage, and their hope, even if their eyes had never seen such a place as Singapore.

I found a quiet corner with seats near another garden; this one filled with tall ferns and the soft sound of trickling water. It reminded me of the cool streams in Hela, where children splash and women wash kaukau, laughing together as they work. Here, there were no women washing, no children playing, yet the presence of green life calmed me. It told me that even in the middle of modern steel and glass, nature still had a place, still offered her comfort.

Nearby, a group of travellers sat with their phones plugged into charging stations. I realised then how dependent people here were on their devices, glowing screens that kept them connected to distant worlds.

I thought of my village, where many homes still lacked electricity, where a phone was often shared by several families, and where charging meant carrying it to the nearest town. In Singapore, power flowed everywhere, like an endless river. For a moment, I felt a pang of shame for my country's struggles. But then I reminded myself that wealth of spirit, community, and culture was also a kind of richness.

As the hours passed, my hunger returned, and I decided to try something else. I found a stall selling satay—grilled meat skewers with peanut sauce. The smell drew me in, smoky and sweet, and when I tasted it, I thought immediately of the times in Hela when we roasted pig over an open fire. The satay was different, smaller pieces, flavoured with spices unknown to me, but the feeling was the same—meat shared, fire tamed, hunger satisfied. Food, I realised again, was a language spoken in every culture, one that connected people beyond words.

I thought too about patience. In Hela, when we cooked in the mumu, we placed everything inside—the pork, kaukau, greens, and bananas—and let the heat of the stones do its work. It was a single act of preparation, followed by waiting.

But here, and later in China, I noticed how each dish was crafted separately, each flavour given its own attention. It showed me a different attitude toward time, a patience that created variety, whereas our cooking showed unity and immediacy. I wondered what that difference revealed about us as peoples—about how we approached life itself.

After eating, I returned once more to the great glass windows overlooking the runways. Night had deepened, and the planes now glowed like fireflies in the darkness. I pressed my forehead against the cool glass and watched one after another lift into the sky, their lights growing smaller until they vanished. Each one carried hundreds of lives, each life carrying dreams, fears, and stories as deep as my own. The thought humbled me, but it also filled me with courage. If others could cross oceans and continents, why not me?

A young woman sat down beside me, dressed smartly in jeans and a white blouse. She smiled and asked in English where I was going. "Beijing," I replied shyly, and she nodded, saying she was flying to Sydney for work. We chatted for a while, and I was struck by her ease, her confidence. She told me she often travelled for business, that airports were like second homes to her. I listened, fascinated, and thought of how different her world was from mine. Yet, in our conversation, I felt a small connection, as if the airport itself had woven us together for a brief moment.

When she left, I sat alone again, but I no longer felt entirely alone. Around me, people moved constantly, each in their own direction, yet somehow sharing the same space, the same waiting, the same anticipation. It was like being part of a *singsing*, where many clans gather, each with their colours, their dances, their drums, yet all united in one great celebration. The airport was its own kind of *singsing*, the song here being the sound of announcements, the beat from rolling suitcases, the dance from the movement of countless feet across polished floors.

By the time the call came for my flight, I was almost reluctant to leave. I had grown attached to this place that was not quite a city and not quite a building, but something in between, something alive with movement. But I gathered my bag, adjusted the bilum slung across my shoulder, and walked toward the gate.

The line moved slowly, and as I waited, I thought again of the journey ahead. Beijing awaited me—a city I had only read about, a place of emperors and revolutions, of walls that stretched across mountains, of people whose language I did not yet know. Fear stirred in me, sharp and quick, but so did determination. I reminded myself of my purpose: to learn, to grow, to bring something back to my people.

As I stepped onto the plane, I whispered a prayer in my heart—for strength, for wisdom, and for safe passage. The attendants greeted me with polite smiles, guiding me to my seat, and soon I was buckled in, staring once more out the window.

The runway lights blurred slightly as my eyes grew heavy. I leaned back, clutching the memory of Singapore tightly. The orchids, the satay, the fountains, the metal birds, the endless movement—all of it would stay with me, part of the story I carried. And as the engines roared and the plane began to rise, I closed my eyes and let the future pull me forward.

The moment the plane lifted from Changi's runway, I pressed my face to the window and watched Singapore shrink into a scatter of lights below. Yet even as the city disappeared, its memory remained vivid within me. Four hours had not been enough to truly know it, but it had been enough to awaken something inside me—a sense of how wide the world was, how many paths stretched out beyond the mountains of Hela, waiting to be walked.

As the plane steadied in the sky, I replayed the images in my mind like a *singsing* unfolding before me. I thought of the orchids in their glass cases, each bloom more delicate than the last, their colours rivaling even the bird-of-paradise plumes worn by Huli men in their bilas. I thought of the great fountain that seemed to fall endlessly from the ceiling, its mist curling in the air like the smoke of our mumu fires. I thought of the satay stall, the sweet taste of candied fruit, the laughter of strangers speaking in languages I could not name.

Each of these memories seemed like gifts placed in my hands—reminders that beauty is not confined to one land, that culture wears many faces. In Hela, beauty is in the mist that rolls across the valley in the early morning, in the painted faces of men dancing with their kundu drums, in the rhythm of women's voices calling children home at sunset. In Singapore, beauty was in polished steel, in glass reflecting the glow of countless lights, in the way the airport itself felt alive, a city within a city. Both worlds were beautiful, though in such different ways.

I smiled, thinking of how my people back home might react if they could see what I had seen. My mother might laugh at the idea of a garden inside a building. My brothers might marvel at the moving walkways that carried people along like magic. My father, I imagined, would stand silently, taking it all in with the steady gaze of a Huli man, before finally nodding as though to say: yes, the world is larger than we thought.

I felt a longing then—not only to carry these stories back to my people one day, but also to find ways of bringing them the opportunities to see such things for themselves. Education had given me the chance to step outside my homeland and walk in another's world. Perhaps, if I worked hard enough, others too would follow. Perhaps one day, a girl from Hela would walk through Changi's halls not with awe alone, but with confidence, knowing she belonged to this greater world.

The hours on the flight passed in a haze of thought. Sometimes I dozed, my dreams a blend of Hela's mountains and Singapore's shining towers. Sometimes I gazed at the dark sky beyond the window, where stars glittered cold and distant, and thought of how small we all are beneath their light. And sometimes I simply sat, my hands resting on the bilum in my lap, feeling the comforting reminder of home.

I remembered, too, the moment I stood by the great glass window in the airport, watching planes lift into the night sky. At the time, I had thought of the *singsings* of my people, where each clan comes dressed in its colours, each beating its drums, each singing its songs, yet all together forming one great harmony. The airport had been like that—its music the rolling of luggage, its song the murmur of countless voices, its dance the footsteps of travellers moving in every direction. And just as in a *singsing*, where the valley becomes alive with energy, the airport had pulsed with a rhythm that made me feel part of something larger.

The memory gave me comfort. I was no longer a frightened girl leaving home for the first time. I was part of a greater *singsing* now, one that stretched across oceans and continents, a *singsing* of humanity itself.

The flight attendants brought trays of food, and when I lifted the cover, I found rice, vegetables, and chicken. It was simple, yet to me it felt like a sign of what awaited me in China—a diet different from Hela's, yet one I would learn to embrace. I thought of how food carries culture, how each bite is more than just taste, but also history, patience, and care. Singapore had already shown me this with its satay, its noodles, its fruits. Now China would show me more.

As the plane pushed northward, I thought of the path that had brought me here. From the valleys of Hela, where I first learned to walk barefoot on soft earth, to the classrooms where I struggled to master English, to the long journey across seas that had brought me to Singapore—I carried it all within me. Each step had prepared me for the next, like stones laid carefully in a garden path.

I whispered a prayer of gratitude—for my family who had encouraged me, for my teachers who had guided me, for the ancestors whose spirits walked with me. Without them, I would not be here, moving toward a new life.

And then, as the engines hummed steadily, I allowed myself to dream of what was to come. Beijing—the capital, the beating heart of China—waited for me. I imagined its wide boulevards, its crowded markets, its ancient palaces and modern skyscrapers standing side by side. I imagined the language that still sounded like music to my ears, mysterious and flowing, which I would one day learn to speak. I imagined the friends I had yet to meet, the lessons I had yet to study, the challenges I had yet to overcome.

For a moment, fear tightened in my chest. What if I failed? What if the language defeated me, or the loneliness became too heavy? But then I thought of Singapore, of how I had walked among strangers and yet found connection, how I had stood in awe but also in strength. If I could navigate that shining maze of glass and light, I could face Beijing too.

The cabin lights dimmed, and most passengers drifted into sleep. I remained awake a little longer, staring out at the stars. They looked the same as they did from Hela—bright points scattered across the black sky. In that moment, I felt a deep truth settle in my heart: no matter how far we travel, the sky above us remains the same. The stars that guided my ancestors across the valleys were the same stars now watching over me as I crossed the seas. I was not lost. I was simply walking a longer path, one that stretched far beyond the mountains, but still led home.

Eventually, my eyes closed, and I slept, the hum of the engines a lullaby. And in my dreams, I walked once more through Singapore, orchids blooming at my side, planes lifting into the sky above, and the voices of countless travellers blending into one great song. It was not the end of my journey, but the beginning. And as dawn approached somewhere beyond the horizon, I carried with me the certainty that I was ready—for Beijing, for China, for whatever awaited me.

The flight from Singapore to Beijing stretched across the skies like a bridge between two worlds, yet to me it felt like a few passing moments. Perhaps it was because my mind refused to rest. I kept thinking about what lay ahead, my heart leaping between excitement and nervousness. I had left Hela, I had left Papua New Guinea, and though Singapore had dazzled me with its order and beauty, I knew that China was the true beginning of this new chapter of my life. It was here I would live, study, struggle, and grow into someone my people could look up to.

As the plane began its descent into Beijing Capital International Airport, I pressed my forehead against the cool window. Below me stretched a sight I had never imagined: roads as wide as rivers, lined with streams of cars moving in perfect order; buildings rising in rows that seemed to stretch beyond the horizon; cranes perched atop unfinished towers, as if the city itself were still being born before my eyes. The scale of it all overwhelmed me. Back home, our mountains stood taller than any structure humans could build, and the valley air was thick with the sound of birds and kundu drums. Here, the noise came from engines, from the hum of a city in motion, and it made me feel both small and awake, like I had stepped into the beating heart of a giant.

When the wheels touched the runway, I felt the jolt run through me. This was it—I had arrived. I was no longer just a Huli woman from the highlands of Papua New Guinea, carrying the weight of six failed scholarship applications and the tears of my mother. I was now a student stepping into one of the world's oldest civilisations, carrying with me both my fears and my unshakable determination.

The airport was unlike anything I had ever seen. It seemed endless, with polished floors that reflected the bright lights above. Signs in bold Chinese characters hung everywhere, but mercifully, English translations followed beneath them. I clutched my bag tightly and followed the stream of travellers, my eyes darting around to take in the strange new world I had entered. There was a faint smell in the air—jet fuel mixed with the sterile scent of cleaning polish and something else, something foreign that I could not name. Even the air conditioning felt different from the humid, earth-scented breezes of home.

I moved through customs slowly, my nervous fingers fumbling with my documents. The officer studied me with a face that revealed nothing, stamped my passport, and waved me through. Just like that, I had entered China. For a brief moment, I wanted to run back, to tell my father that perhaps this was too much for me, that perhaps I had flown too far from the safety of the valley. But then I remembered his words: *"You must go. You must see what the world holds. Bring something back for your people."* Those words steadied me as I lifted my chin and walked into the arrivals hall.

The hall itself was a sea of faces. People waited with flowers, with balloons, with tired eyes fixed on the sliding doors that released new arrivals like myself. My own eyes scanned the crowd nervously until they found a young man holding a piece of paper. On it, in bold letters, were the words: "Papua New Guinea students." My heart leapt. That was me. That was us. I was not alone.

When he saw us, his face broke into a warm smile, and he waved with the energy of someone genuinely happy to see us. That small gesture dissolved some of my fear. He introduced himself in careful English as our student guide, assigned to help us settle in. He was patient, gathering us together like a shepherd collecting a scattered flock, and led us out of the hall into the cool Beijing air.

The first breath I took outside the airport shocked me. It was colder than I expected, a crisp bite in the wind that made me pull my jacket tighter around me. The sky was not the blue of home but a pale grey, the light diffused and heavy, as though the city wore a veil. I climbed onto the bus waiting for us, and as it pulled away, I pressed my face once more against the glass, eager not to miss a single detail.

The ride into Beijing was my true introduction to China. Wide avenues stretched before us, lined with rows of trees. Cars honked, bicycles weaved between them fearlessly, and pedestrians crossed the streets with an ease that suggested they had long mastered the rhythm of such a place. Skyscrapers rose into the sky like mountains of steel and glass, but tucked between them I caught glimpses of older neighborhoods, their tiled roofs and narrow lanes whispering of another time. It was as though the past and present lived side by side, each refusing to give way entirely to the other.

I thought of Hela as the bus rolled on. In my home, life followed the rhythm of the land. We measured time by the growth of kaukau and the passing of the rainy season, not by the blinking of traffic lights. Here, everything seemed to move faster, sharper, louder. Yet, strangely, I did not feel pushed away. Instead, I felt drawn in, as though the city itself was daring me to keep up, to prove that a Huli woman from the highlands could find her place among the towers of Beijing.

The days that followed deepened this feeling of awe and unease. At the university campus, I met other students from Papua New Guinea, some of whom had already learned a little Mandarin. They seemed more at ease, but I struggled. The language was a wall I kept crashing into. In class, when professors spoke, their voices became a blur of tones I could not untangle. At times I felt like a child again, reduced to guessing meanings from gestures and expressions. There were nights I lay in bed fighting tears, wondering if I had been foolish to come.

But the kindness of people softened the sharp edges of my struggle. My teachers were patient, my classmates generous with their help. I began to pick out words here and there, like stars slowly appearing in a dark sky. The breakthrough came unexpectedly.

One afternoon, as I walked across campus, two Chinese students passed me, speaking quickly. I caught a few words and realised, to my shock, that I understood them. Only weeks earlier, their conversation would have been meaningless noise, but now it carried sense. That small victory lit a fire in me. If I could understand a few words, then I could understand more. If I could say a few sentences, then one day I could speak with ease.

My guide took us into the city often in those first weeks, and each outing revealed more of Beijing's character. I saw the Forbidden City, its red walls and golden roof shimmering in the sunlight, a reminder of China's ancient power. I stood in Tiananmen Square, feeling the weight of history pressing down on the vast open space. I wandered through hutongs, the narrow alleys where daily life unfolded with the smell of food and the sound of laughter. Each place seemed to tell a story, and I listened, even when I could not understand every word.

Food, too, became a teacher. In Beijing, meals were an event, a gathering. Dishes of every colour and flavour filled the table, each one carefully prepared, each one reflecting patience and precision. Compared to the single-dish mumu of my Hela home, where kaukau, taro, greens, and pork were cooked together beneath hot stones, these Chinese meals spoke of a different attitude toward food—an attention to variety, to detail, to an harmony of taste. At first, it overwhelmed me. Later, it fascinated me. I realised that food itself carried culture, carrying within it the values of a people. In China, food taught me patience. At home, food taught me resilience.

Every day in Beijing stretched me in new directions. I stumbled, I learned, I grew. Slowly, I began to find confidence in small things: ordering food in Mandarin, navigating the bus system, greeting my teachers with respect in their own language. I learned to bow my head slightly, to pass papers with both hands, to say "xièxiè" with sincerity. Each of these gestures was a thread, weaving me into the fabric of life here.

Yet I never forgot who I was. On some nights, as fireworks exploded during festivals, I thought of the *singsings* of my people, the bright headdresses and the painted faces, the chants and the drums that carried across the valley. Those memories kept me grounded. I was far from Hela, but Hela lived in me. It gave me strength when the city threatened to swallow me whole.

Looking back, I see that my arrival in Beijing was not just about stepping off a plane into a new country. It was about stepping into a new version of myself. I came trembling, uncertain, burdened by my past failures. But I walked forward anyway, guided by hope, by my father's words, by the vision of what I could bring back to my people. Beijing did not make it easy, but it made me stronger. In the end, the city did not erase the Huli woman in me—it sharpened me, taught me to see myself more clearly, and gave me the courage to keep walking, no matter how vast or foreign the world became.

At Beijing Language and Culture University (BLCU), I still remember the weight of the air the day our bus rolled through the gates. It was late summer, and Beijing's sky was pale with haze, the kind that makes the sun appear soft and distant. As we drove past the great archway that marked the entrance to the campus, my chest tightened, not with fear exactly, but with the strange heaviness that comes when you realise you are stepping into a new life.

The university grounds stretched wide and orderly before us. Trees lined the roads in neat rows, unlike the wild, uneven forests of home. The buildings rose tall and square, their walls painted white and gray, like silent guardians watching over the thousands of young people who passed through them each year. I had never seen a campus like this in Papua New Guinea. There, our universities felt scattered and familiar, our spaces shaped by the bend of the mountains and the paths of rivers. But here, in Beijing, every road seemed to run straight, every tree was planted in deliberate symmetry.

When the bus stopped, we were not left to wander in confusion. A group of people stood waiting for us, their faces breaking into warm smiles as we stepped down one by one. They were not strangers, though we had never met them before. They were staff from the Papua New Guinea Embassy in Beijing, which we called Kundu Haus. The name alone was a balm. A kundu drum carries the heartbeat of our people; when it is struck, it binds us to the land, to each other, to the voices of our ancestors. To know that our embassy here bore that name meant that even in this foreign land of towering buildings and endless roads, we had a heartbeat that was ours.

Their presence reassured me. I had felt a little like a single leaf carried on the wind, blown far from the valley where my feet first learned to walk. But seeing them, hearing the familiar tones of Tok Pisin and English mixed with the laughter of my countrymen; I knew I was not lost. I was not abandoned. My people were here, watching over us, carrying us forward.

The very next thing that struck me at BLCU was the sheer diversity that filled the campus. I had grown up in the Huli land of Tari, where life revolved around the rhythms of clan and garden. Everyone I knew shared the same skin, the same language, the same customs. Our differences were measured in subtle ways—who your father was, which ridge your clan lived on, which songs your mother taught you.

Diversity for us meant the neighbouring tribes: the Duna, the Enga, the Hagen people. We distinguished them by their accents, their dances, the shells they wore during ceremonies.

But Beijing was another universe entirely. It was not just one or two neighboring tribes; it was the whole world in one place.

On that first day, I watched in amazement as students from Africa walked past in bright clothes of green, yellow, and orange, their voices carrying rhythms that seemed to dance in the air. I saw Europeans with skin so pale it seemed to glow in the afternoon light, some with hair like fire, others with hair like strands of straw. I saw students from the Middle East in long robes, their words curling like smoke as they spoke. I saw young people from every part of Asia, each with their own languages and faces, their own ways of carrying themselves.

It was overwhelming, but also beautiful. It was as if the world had cracked open, spilling its people into this one campus. For the first time in my life, I understood what it meant to live in a global community. We were young, all of us, carrying our flags in our hearts, carrying the pride of our families, carrying the hope of our nations.

The air buzzed with languages. I heard English spoken in accents I could barely recognise, French rising and falling like music, Spanish rolling fast and smooth, Arabic flowing like water, and the clicking sounds of African tongues. Everywhere I turned, the campus was alive with sound. I smelled spices drifting from the cafeteria, dishes I had never seen before. I saw flags pinned to clothes, national costumes displayed with pride. The place was like a market of humanity, but instead of buying and selling, we were exchanging knowledge, culture, and stories.

That evening, I pulled out my small notebook. I had carried it with me from home, its cover already worn from being opened too many times. Writing had always been my way of holding onto moments before they slipped away. I sat beneath a tree and tried to capture the scene before me. The words came as a poem, unpolished but true:

You and me, from one world,
We travel far, for a thousand miles,
Meeting in Beijing.

It was more than just poetry. It was a truth I was living.

That scholarship was not only about studying in China—it was about being part of something larger than myself. It was about stepping into a world where knowledge was not just individual but collective, where young people from every corner of the planet could meet, exchange ideas, and form friendships that crossed borders.

Sometimes, when I think back, I marvel at the courage of that younger version of myself. For a Huli woman, raised in the highlands of Papua New Guinea, to fly across oceans, to step into Beijing, to sit in lecture halls with people from fifty different nations—it was something my grandmothers could never have imagined.

I carried with me the voice of my mother, reminding me that as a Huli woman, I was a daughter of the land. My hands were meant to dig sweet potato gardens, to tend to pigs, to cook food on open fires, to weave bilums. Yet here I was, with pen and paper instead of digging stick, notebooks instead of gardens, classrooms instead of ridges.

In Beijing, lying on the narrow dormitory bed, I would close my eyes and see the ridges of Tari. I would hear the rustle of pitpit grass, the squeal of pigs, the voices of children running along the ridges. I would smell the smoke of burning firewood clinging to my bilum. Then I would open my eyes and see concrete walls, fluorescent lights, and the soft buzz of students walking past in slippers.

This was the new garden I had been planted in. And like any Huli woman, I had to learn how to tend it, to make it grow.

At BLCU, I quickly learned that being from Papua New Guinea made me both invisible and visible at the same time.

Many students did not know where my country was. Some asked if it was in Africa. Others confused it with Guinea, Guyana, or even Hawaii. Each time, I would take a deep breath, smile, and explain: *"Papua New Guinea is in the Pacific, north of Australia. We are one of the most diverse countries in the world, with more than 800 languages."*

The more I explained, the more I realised that my presence here was important. I was not only studying for myself. I was representing my people. My voice, my accent, my face—all of these carried the story of the Huli, of Papua New Guinea, of a land many had never heard of. It was humbling.

Of course, not everything was easy. I struggled with the food at first. Rice was common enough, but many dishes were oily or spicy in ways my body was not used to. I longed for sweet potatoes baked in the earth, for taro boiled in clay pots, for greens cooked with coconut cream. I missed the taste of pork, roasted over hot stones.

The weather, too, was strange. The air in Beijing was dry and sometimes heavy with smog. My throat often felt sore, my skin cracked. I missed the moist air of the highlands, the way mist rolled over the ridges in the morning.

But slowly, I adapted. I learned to eat noodles with chopsticks, fumbling at first, laughing with others at my mistakes. I learned to drink hot water, which Chinese people preferred over cold. I learned to carry a mask on days when the smog grew thick.

Despite the small struggles, the greatest gift of BLCU was the sense of belonging to a global family. In the evenings, students gathered in common spaces to talk, to sing, to share food. I remember one night when a group of African students cooked a meal and invited us all to taste it. Another evening, we gathered to dance—each group teaching the others steps from their homelands. I showed them a simple Huli rhythm, clapping and stamping as we do back home. They laughed, they tried, and for a moment, the world felt like a village.

I came to see that, despite our differences, we shared the same dream: to learn, to succeed, to return home and make a difference.

Our time at BLCU was brief. Soon we would all disperse to our respective universities across China. Some would fly, others would take the long trains that stretched across provinces. I was to travel south, to Wuhan in Hubei Province, a city I had only heard of in passing but would soon come to know intimately.

But before I left Beijing, I took one last evening to sit under a tree on campus, notebook in hand. The air was cool, filled with the chatter of students passing by, their voices blending into a soft chorus of languages. I opened my notebook and wrote, not a poem this time, but a promise: *This is only the beginning.*

I did not know then all the challenges that lay ahead—loneliness, culture shock, the long winters, the moments of doubt. But I also did not know the joy that would come: the friendships, the discoveries, the pride of learning a new language, the strength of carrying my people's story into classrooms where it had never been heard before.

BLCU was more than just a starting point. It was a mirror, showing me who I was in the eyes of the world, and who I could become. It was the place where I first understood that my journey was not just my own—it was for my family, my people, my land.

And as I closed my notebook that night, I felt the weight of the kundu drum in my heart, steady and strong, reminding me that wherever I went, I carried the sound of home.

5

A FIRST GLIMPSE OF THE FORBIDDEN CITY

When I first saw the gates of the Forbidden City, I felt as if my breath had been caught in the fist of some enormous ancestor who had waited for me to come across the oceans and mountains to witness what his hands had once built. I had walked many roads before, through the ridges of our highlands where the mists curl like restless spirits, where the bright feathers of birds-of-paradise sit upon our men's heads, where the paint and ochre on the skin say, "I am here, I am alive." But here, in this city of red walls and golden roofs, I felt myself shrink and expand at the same time. My legs remembered the mud tracks of Koroba, the slippery stones in the rivers where we wash, the cracked heels of our mothers, the ash that sticks on our calves when the fires burn low. Yet my eyes were drawn upward, always upward, to the sharp yet smooth sweep of the roofs, to the dragons curling like smoke across the beams, to the endless symmetry that seemed like a song without a single false note.

The air that morning was bright but dry, the kind of sunlight that presses down without the heavy touch of humidity. It was different from the mountain light I knew, softer there, filtered through mist and cloud, breaking itself into shafts like the ribs of a spirit. Here the sky was clean, sharp, and almost pitiless. Every line of the roof caught fire in that sun, every glazed tile glowed as if it had been polished just for me. I squinted, though I wanted my eyes wide open, not to miss even a corner of this wonder. My body felt small, not in shame, but in the way a child feels small in the presence of elders — small and therefore ready to learn.

I was not born among stone and tile. I was born where the houses lean on stilts above wet soil, where the roofs are patched with kunai grass, where every wall remembers the smoke of years. I grew up with the rhythm of pigs grunting, men shouting, women laughing with heavy bilums across their foreheads, children clapping their hands against the rain. Our world is not built for the eyes of emperors. It is built for hunger and laughter, for grief and marriage, for the sound of birds and the silence after a death. And yet, standing before the Meridian Gate, I felt as though the builders of this palace had also known hunger and laughter and silence, but they had lifted them into heaven, pressing them into gold tiles and painted beams, turning their memory into something permanent.

The courtyard was vast, so vast that my own voice inside me seemed to stumble and lose its way. In my village, when you step out of your house, you can hear someone's cough, someone's axe against wood, someone's baby crying. Here, even surrounded by tourists, there was a strange emptiness, a space that no one could fill. The flagstones stretched like a dry river, each slab wider than my chest, each joint running away from me like roads into the horizon. My feet ached already, though I had only begun to walk, and I thought of the women of my clan pacing back and forth on garden paths, balancing heavy firewood across their foreheads, never stopping, never complaining. Perhaps if they stood here, their steps would echo as mine did, sounding thin against the hugeness of stone.

I thought of the ancestors of this place, of emperors who would step through gates with thousands of soldiers, thousands of servants, and yet the stones beneath my feet still seemed to echo with a deeper silence, a silence that belonged not to the crowd but to time itself. It was not emptiness, but fullness too heavy for voices to rise above.

I touched the red walls. The paint was smooth, my fingers sliding as though across skin made new every day. In my home, walls carry the ridges of hands, the grooves of knives cutting wood, the stains of betel nut spit.

Here, the wall was not just a wall. It was an announcement. It was saying, "I am strong. I will not fade." My grandmother used to say that walls listen, that they catch whispers and keep them. If these walls have been listening for centuries, what voices have they swallowed? What sighs of concubines, what laughter of children hidden in courtyards, what orders of men whose words could cost lives?

As I pressed my palm against the wall, it was cool, almost cold despite the sun. Stone holds memory differently from earth. Earth warms quickly; it crumbles, it breathes with us. But stone is stubborn. It keeps its chill even when the day is hot, as if it refuses to belong entirely to the living. My skin shivered and I pulled back, though I longed to keep touching, to take into myself the secret of that endurance.

I walked slowly, because rushing would have been disrespectful. Every roof corner had an animal carved in watch, dragons and lions, creatures whose eyes seemed alive even though they were frozen. Their teeth gleamed white, their claws ready to strike, though their bodies would never move. I thought of the spirits we call out to in our *singsings*, the shadows that sit at the edge of firelight. Those are spirits of forest and earth, always near, always half-seen. But here, the guardians had been carved, fixed forever in position, made into a discipline. I wondered if their spirits had agreed to this stillness, or if they were trapped like birds in cages, powerful but never free.

The Forbidden City smelled different from any place I had ever been. Not of pigs and smoke and damp grass, but of stone warmed by sun, of dust settled into the cracks, of tourists' perfumes mingling with something older that I could not name. My nose was confused. It wanted to return to the comfort of firewood and sweet potatoes, but it was being asked to learn another story, one told in lacquer and tile. Sometimes the wind brought a faint trace of incense from a nearby shrine, and that smoke pulled at me, reminding me of the way our own men burn leaves to speak with spirits. Smoke is a bridge in every land, I thought. It carries words we cannot say aloud.

I remember looking at the roof ridges shining like they carried the last rays of all the suns that had ever set upon them. Gold—more gold than my eyes had ever believed could exist. Not the gold of jewelry in town shops, not the gold of coins or trinkets, but gold that seemed to declare itself as part of the sky. My people know the shimmer of bird feathers, the bright red of hibiscus, the rich blue of mountains in the distance. But this was another kind of shimmer, one that made you aware of your smallness, one that told you that someone once decided to catch sunlight and command it to sit upon his house forever.

I walked through halls with names that tasted strange in my mouth. The Hall of Supreme Harmony. The Hall of Central Harmony. The Hall of Preserving Harmony. Harmony, always harmony, as if the builders feared its loss so much, they carved the word into every space. In my village, harmony is not carved. It is fought for in gardens, in quarrels, in bride price, in pigs exchanged, in songs sung until voices crack. Harmony is fragile, always at the edge of breaking.

I wondered if even here, with walls so thick, with roofs so heavy, with names carved so deeply, harmony had not also been fragile. Perhaps it is fragile everywhere.

I climbed steps worn down by centuries of feet. Each step dipped slightly in the middle where heels had struck and struck again, a thousand times. I felt myself adding to that wear, just a grain of dust on the mountain of time. My breath grew heavier, but I welcomed it. The climb felt like a ritual, each step asking me whether I truly wished to see further, each stone testing my resolve. At the top I looked back, and the courtyards spread like layers of a story unfolding behind me.

Tourists snapped their cameras, their voices rising and falling in many languages. Some wore hats with brims so wide they looked like giant leaves. Others held umbrellas though no rain was falling, afraid of the sun. Children darted between their parents, laughing, tugging, whining. A woman from somewhere far away touched the wall as I had, her face lit with the same wonder. And in that moment, I realised the Forbidden City was not only for the emperors, nor only for China, but for all of us who carried eyes and hearts. It had become a meeting place of strangers who did not share language but shared awe.

But I carried inside me the voice of my grandmother, who never saw anything beyond our valleys, who used to tell me that the world was larger than our eyes could bear, and that if ever I walked far, I should not forget the smell of sweet potato roasting in the earth. I carried her with me as I stepped over stones smoothed by millions of footsteps. I wanted to tell her, "Grandmother, they built houses here so wide that ten of our houses could fit side by side inside one hall. They painted their beams with dragons that seem to move when you stare. They carved lions who still guard though the emperors are long dead." She would laugh, perhaps, and say, "Even the greatest houses cannot keep death away." And she would be right.

Yet I could not deny the beauty. My heart swelled as if it were dancing, though my feet were only walking. I thought of our *singsings*, where men beat the kundu drum, where feathers shake, where bodies paint themselves into living art. That beauty lives only for the day. By morning, the paint has faded, the feathers have been laid down, the songs are only echoes. But here, the beauty has been made to last centuries. It is another kind of *singsing*, one stretched across time, one that continues even when the dancers have long left.

There was one courtyard where I stopped, letting the crowd pass. The shadows of the roof edges fell across the stone, sharp and clean. A bird flew overhead, its wings a brief blur. For a moment, I imagined what it would be like to live inside these walls, not as a visitor but as one of those whose life was bound to this place. I thought of the women who must have looked up at the same roof, who must have walked the same courtyards, who must have longed for the freedom of that bird. My chest grew heavy. Beauty can also be a prison.

I rested a moment on the low step, feeling the hardness of the stone press into me. I remembered how, at home, we sit on the ground softened by grass, our thighs warmed by the earth itself. This stone gave no comfort, no yielding. It was built not for rest but for endurance. And I thought—maybe this was the truth of emperors. To sit always on stone, never on soil. To be cut off from the soft warmth of the earth, always lifted above it.

As I walked, I listened with my skin. The stones were speaking. They said, "We have seen emperors rise and fall. We have seen blood spilled and laughter echoed. We have seen hands polish us, wash us, repair us. We have seen the years march like soldiers. And still we remain." Their voice was deep, almost beyond hearing, but it moved through my bones. In our land, the soil also speaks. When we dig, it tells us whether the sweet potato will grow well, whether the rain will be kind. But it never claims permanence. It accepts its own cycles. Here, the stones claimed to outlast even memory.

I thought of my own body. It will wrinkle, bend, break. My hands will lose their strength. My breath will leave me. But my eyes, in that moment, had been given a gift, to see something built to resist death. And I thought, maybe that is what people everywhere want: to resist death, to leave behind a mark so large that the sky itself cannot ignore it.

I reached the throne room, where the dragon throne sat high, behind layers of steps. It was roped off, guarded, unreachable. Yet my heart raced as if it were something alive, as if I had stumbled upon the beating heart of a mountain. I could not see the emperor, but I could imagine him, robes heavy, voice echoing, eyes trained to see everything yet nothing. I wondered if he was happy. Power, my grandmother always said, is a pig too big to carry. It will crush you if you are not careful. Looking at that throne, I felt the weight of centuries, of decisions, of lives changed with a word. I pitied the man who once sat there, even as I marveled at the beauty of his seat.

When I stepped outside again, the sunlight fell upon the many rooves, turning them into fire. I thought of my land, of the fire that crackles in every house, of the small flames that keep us warm, that cook our food, that light our nights. This fire was different, untouchable, far above my head. Yet both fires, great and small, told the same story: we humans cannot live without light.

I left the Forbidden City slowly, as though tearing myself from a dream. My heart was full, too full. I wanted to run back to my people and tell them, to sing it, to paint it on my skin, to show with my hands what my tongue could never fully describe. I wanted to say, "I have seen a city within walls, a city that once held the heart of an empire, a city where stone and wood have been taught to live forever." And yet I also wanted to say, "I walked there as myself, a Huli woman, and I carried my land with me, and my land whispered back to me through every tile and every stone."

Even now, when I close my eyes, I see those roofs against the sky. I hear the silence of the courtyards. I feel the smooth red wall beneath my fingers. And I know that my first impression was not just of beauty, not just of wonder, but of the strange closeness of all peoples. For though I come from mud walls and kunai grass, and they built palaces of tile and stone, we both are trying to make our lives mean something more than breath and hunger. We both carve our dreams into the world.

That is what I learned from the Forbidden City. That beauty can be a song stretched across centuries. That power can be as heavy as gold tiles. That silence can speak. And that even a woman from the highlands of Papua New Guinea can find herself mirrored in the stones of China, as if the world itself had always meant for us to meet.

PART II

LIFE IN A NEW WORLD

6

SETTLING IN WUHAN

When I first saw the name "Wuhan" printed on my scholarship placement letter, I stared at it as though the paper itself carried a secret I could not yet decipher. The word seemed strange, heavy with distance, not belonging to the geography of my childhood. It was not like Tari, my home in the Hela highlands, whose very sound carried the weight of ridges and mist, of pigs squealing in their pens, of voices lifted in *singsing* under the mountain moon.

Wuhan, instead, was a name from faraway maps, from newspaper stories, from the imagination of a young girl who had grown up hearing of other lands but never setting foot on them. All I knew from the few things I had read was that it sat on the great Yangtze River, somewhere in the center of China, and that it would be my home for the next chapter of my journey.

That letter was both a gift and a burden. It was a gift because it held the promise of education, of new horizons, of knowledge I could carry back like sweet potato from a rich garden. It was a burden because it pulled me away from everything familiar—my family, my language, my land—and dropped me into a place where I would have to grow roots in foreign soil.

A Huli woman belongs to her clan, to her land, to her pigs. Our lives are interwoven like the strands of a bilum. But this scholarship was asking me to leave that bilum behind and weave a new one, far from the soil of Hela.

The day we boarded the train from Beijing to Wuhan, I felt both excitement and fear pressing against my ribs. Beijing had already overwhelmed me with its size, its endless crowds, its subway trains that roared like underground rivers. Now, we were to travel deeper into China, to a city none of us really knew. The railway station in Beijing was itself an ocean of humanity. Enormous halls stretched in every direction, filled with travellers dragging suitcases, children clinging to their parents, vendors shouting, screens flashing departure times. It felt as though half the country was on the move, each person carrying a story, a destination, a dream.

When the train finally slid out of the station, I pressed my forehead to the glass and watched Beijing's towering skyline give way to villages, fields, and mountains. The speed was unlike anything I had experienced before. Back home, our PMVs groaned along the Highlands Highway, bumping over potholes, swerving around landslides. Here, the train glided as smoothly as a bird in flight, covering in minutes what would take us hours back home. I thought of my people walking for hours to reach markets, of my mother carrying kaukau in her bilum to trade, of children trudging to school. And here I was, flying across a country larger than I had ever imagined, chasing knowledge that I hoped would one day feed those very children.

Hours passed, the scenery shifting like pages in a storybook. Vast rice fields stretched to the horizon. Rivers twisted like silver snakes. Villages clustered with tiled rooftops, smoke curling into the air. Then factories, chimneys rising like fingers, pouring clouds into the sky. Each scene reminded me how immense this country truly was. By the time the train slowed into Wuhan, my heart was pounding with anticipation.

We stepped off at Hankou Station, and immediately the air wrapped itself around me like a wet blanket. The humidity was heavy, clinging to my skin until I felt sticky and tired. It was summer, and the heat seemed to rise from the very concrete itself. The station swirled with noise and motion: announcements crackling over loudspeakers, porters rushing with luggage, families reuniting in noisy embraces. I gripped the handle of my suitcase tightly, afraid of being swept away in the tide.

But then, out of the crowd, I saw three familiar figures— Papua New Guinean students, waiting to welcome us. Their voices, carrying the rhythm of Tok Pisin and the warmth of home, cut through the chaos like the sound of kundu drums in the distance. Relief flooded me. In that instant, I realised how deeply I needed the comfort of my own people, even here in this faraway city.

Wuhan revealed itself to me slowly, like a book opening one chapter at a time. The city was divided by two mighty rivers— the Yangtze and the Han—and linked by bridges that gleamed under the sun. Everywhere I looked, there was motion: buses rumbling down wide boulevards, bicycles weaving like fish through traffic, vendors calling out cheerfully, selling fruits, skewers of meat, steaming bowls of noodles.

Coming from Port Moresby, Wuhan felt enormous. Not only was it a political and cultural center, but it was also an industrial heart, home to the Wuhan Iron and Steel Corporation, a name I had only ever heard in textbooks. At night, the city glowed with neon lights reflecting off the river waters, dazzling my eyes and making me feel both exhilarated and deeply homesick.

The next day, classes began at Central China Normal University. Unlike back home, where the first week is often spent easing into routines, here there was no delay. From the very first hour, I was immersed in Mandarin. The teachers spoke with passion and speed, their voices flowing like rushing rivers, only occasionally throwing in an English word.

I quickly realised how little I understood. When classmates laughed at a joke, I sat silently, smiling without comprehension.

When instructions were given, I struggled to follow. Even simple tasks—ordering food in the cafeteria, asking for directions, greeting the gate guards—became monumental challenges.

Frustration soon crept in. There were nights when I lay awake in my dormitory, staring at the ceiling fan spinning lazily, wondering if I had made a mistake coming here. I missed Tok Pisin. I missed the ease of English. I missed the voices of my people, the warmth of my clan. I missed being able to express myself without stumbling over syllables that felt foreign on my tongue.

But slowly, something shifted. I reminded myself why I was here. This scholarship was not just a piece of paper; it was the fruit of sacrifice—my own, my family's, my country's. It was a chance to carry knowledge back to my homeland, to help children in classrooms that too often went without teachers, to light a path for other young women from Hela who dreamed of something more. If Thomas Edison could endure thousands of failures before creating the light bulb, could I not endure these daily humiliations until I improved?

I began carrying a small notebook everywhere. Whenever I heard a new word, I jotted it down. I practiced speaking with shopkeepers, no matter how many times they corrected me. I laughed at my own mistakes, turning embarrassment into fuel. Slowly, the sounds began to make sense. The first time I managed to order a meal without confusion, the pride I felt was greater than if I had passed an exam.

One of the most fascinating yet difficult classes was Shufa—Chinese calligraphy. At first, the brush felt strange in my hand, and my strokes wobbled like the legs of a newborn piglet. My characters looked messy, nothing like the elegant lines of my teacher's.

But as I practiced, I began to see that calligraphy was not just about writing—it was about patience, balance, and respect for tradition. Each stroke carried history, each character a meaning deeper than its shape. As I dipped the brush in ink and tried again and again, I realised that this discipline was teaching me not only a new skill but also a new way of seeing the world.

Life on campus was vibrant and challenging. The grounds were expansive, with dormitories rising like towers, lecture halls filled with eager students, gardens blooming with flowers, and sports fields buzzing with activity.

The canteen was always crowded, the air thick with the aroma of rice, noodles, and spices that sometimes burned my tongue. At first, the food felt alien. Soups that smelled unfamiliar, dishes so spicy they made my eyes water, dumplings I wasn't sure how to eat. But slowly, I developed a taste for it. Before long, I was craving Wuhan's specialty—hot dry noodles, a dish that became my comfort food in the midst of homesickness.

Despite the language barrier, friendships began to blossom. Some classmates were curious about Papua New Guinea, a country they had rarely heard of. They asked me about our culture, our customs, our land. I told them about the Huli, about the wigmen who grow their hair in sacred seclusion, about our *singsings* where tribes gather in a sea of feathers and paint, about the bilum that carries not just food but the stories of our women. In return, they shared their own traditions, their dialects, their family recipes. We laughed together, stumbled through conversations mixing English, Mandarin, and gestures, and slowly built bridges across our differences.

Wuhan was not easy, but it was transformative. It tested me in ways I had never expected. It humbled me when I failed to speak, when I felt lost in the crowd. It lifted me when I succeeded, when I finally strung together a sentence that someone understood. It showed me that resilience is not about avoiding hardship but about enduring it, learning from it, and growing stronger through it.

By the end of that year, I could hold basic conversations in Mandarin. I could write characters with some confidence. I could walk through the city without fear, order food without hesitation, and even joke with classmates in a language that had once felt impossible. Wuhan became more than a city where I studied Chinese—it became the furnace where my perseverance was tested and refined, where I discovered that a Huli woman could carry her strength even into the heart of a foreign land.

When the time came to leave for Tianjin, I stood once more at the railway station, my suitcase by my side, my heart heavy with farewell. Wuhan had been my first real test, my first big school of resilience. As the train pulled away, I whispered to myself the promise I had written one evening under a tree on campus: "This is only the beginning."

7

RIDING THE FUTURE: MY FIRST DRIVERLESS TAXI IN WUHAN

When I first heard people in Wuhan talking about taxis that drove themselves, I thought they were joking. Back home in Hela, a vehicle without a driver would sound like a spirit story — something our elders might whisper about by the fire. I laughed when I first heard it, but inside I felt uneasy too. The idea of a car that moves without human hands, that decides its own path, that sees without eyes — it felt like a story from another world.

Where I come from, a man who drives a PMV or a truck is someone we look up to. Driving is not just work — it's bravery. Our roads twist through mountains and mud, the rivers rise without warning, the clouds drop rain heavy as stone. You must know the feel of the earth beneath the tyres, the sound of water under the bridge. You must listen to the wind and trust your gut. To drive is to stay alive. And yet here I was, far from the land that raised me, standing on a busy Wuhan street, about to ride in a taxi that needed no driver at all.

The first time I saw it, I froze. A small white car, silent and smooth, gliding toward the curb like a dream. It looked like any other car — but empty. No one behind the wheel, no face looking back at me. I clutched my bilum tight against my chest. My mother had told me, before I left for China, "Carry something from home. It will keep you safe." I felt the bilum's rough fibres between my fingers and whispered a prayer to steady my heart.

When the door opened with a soft hiss, I hesitated. My feet felt heavy, as if my spirit refused to move. What if the car failed to see me? What if it ran into someone? I remembered my elders' teachings: the earth is your teacher, the hand of a person your safest guide. But another voice inside me — the one that had pushed me to cross the ocean and study here — whispered, "Go on. See what the world has become."

So, I stepped inside.

The air was cool, faintly perfumed. The seats were soft and pale, the windows clean and wide. A screen lit up before me, showing a map and a small glowing dot — me. A calm voice spoke in Mandarin, words I only half understood, announcing our route. I looked at the space where the driver should be, and saw only the curve of the steering wheel turning on its own, steady and sure. My fingers gripped the seat. My heart beat fast, but I didn't want to show fear — not to the machine, not to myself.

When the car began to move, my breath caught. It rolled forward so gently, as if testing the ground before trusting it. The city outside was alive — bicycles flashing by, buses sighing to a stop, people hurrying through rain-scented air. I watched everything as if I were a child again, learning the world anew. Each sound felt sharper, each light brighter.

In Hela, we survive by control — by reading the land and taking charge of the road beneath us. But here, I was asked to let go. I could not steer; I could not brake. I could only watch, breathe, and trust. It was like floating on a river you do not know, carried by a current unseen. I whispered another prayer, not only for safety, but for understanding.

At the first intersection, a man suddenly ran across the road, holding a child's hand. The car slowed instantly, smooth as breath, and let them pass. My whole body tensed, ready for impact, but it never came. The car had already seen them — or sensed them — and adjusted. I felt wonder rise inside me, soft and trembling. How could something made of metal and wire read the chaos of human life so calmly?

I thought of my uncles back home, gripping their steering wheels with strength and pride, reacting to every bump, every turn. Their skill was human, alive, instinctive. This machine's skill was something else — quiet, precise, patient. Its patience humbled me.

As we moved, I found myself whispering softly, "Take me safely. Watch for the people." The car did not answer in words, but it seemed to hear. It flowed through traffic with steady grace, stopping where needed, slowing when someone drifted into its path. I realised that trust — real trust — is not blind. It grows through observation, through watching and seeing that the other holds your safety in its hands.

Outside, Wuhan buzzed with life. Motorbikes weaved like dragonflies. Old women sold fruit on corners. The air smelled of rain, dumplings, and the sharp tang of electricity. The car glided through it all, unhurried, balanced, alive. I remembered the rivers of Tari, brown and strong, winding around rocks and tree roots, never fighting the land but moving with it. This car, too, moved like a river — bending, flowing, adapting. It was made by humans, yet it behaved with nature's wisdom.

My fear began to soften. I watched how the machine moved, how it slowed before turns, how it paused when people crossed. I could feel my shoulders loosen, my breath deepen. Surrender no longer felt like weakness. It felt like peace. Back home, we say that to walk with the land, you must stop fighting it. Perhaps the same is true with life — and even with machines.

Each ride after that became like meditation. I began to observe the small details: how the screen displayed the world around us, how the sensors blinked when we approached an intersection, how the car anticipated danger before I could even see it. I began to think about the people who had built it — the engineers who stayed up through the night, testing and fixing, teaching this machine how to move safely among us. I imagined their care, their attention, their patience. And I thought, perhaps care itself is the soul of technology.

When rain fell, the streets glowed like wet silk. Umbrellas bloomed like flowers, bicycles splashed through puddles, and neon lights reflected on the ground, like stars caught in water. I thought the car would struggle, but it did not. It slowed when it should, stopped when it must, continued when safe. Watching it, I felt something deep: mastery is not about control, it is about understanding. The car did not fight the chaos — it moved with it. Like a wise elder, it waited for the right moment, then acted.

I began to think of the lessons this machine was teaching me. Back home, when we plant kaukau, we watch the soil, the clouds, the insects. We do not rush. We wait for signs.

Here, this car too waited for signs — signals, sensors, the subtle movement of people. It was different, but the same. I began to see that learning is not only from land or people. It can come from creation itself — from what humans make when they work with patience and foresight.

Each ride taught me something new. I learned that anticipation is another form of kindness. That precision is another form of respect. That slowing down can be a sign of wisdom, not weakness. I began to see parallels between this city's roads and the pathways of life — full of motion, uncertainty, and moments where trust must replace control.

Sometimes, as I rode, I would close my eyes. I would feel the hum of the car beneath me, soft as a heartbeat, and I would let my thoughts drift back to Hela. I would see my mother bent over her garden, her hands deep in the soil. I would hear my brothers laughter near the river, the sound of axes in the forest, the smell of smoke from cooking fires. I would think of how far I had come — from muddy mountain tracks to the clean, ordered roads of Wuhan. And I would realise that learning to trust this driverless taxi was also learning to trust life itself.

Once, a child's red ball rolled onto the road. The car saw it before I did. It slowed, curved, and glided around it without a sound. I smiled, amazed. The car had not only seen the ball — it had understood the meaning behind it. A child must be nearby. It moved with empathy, though it had no heart. That thought stayed with me. Machines may not feel as we do, but they can still act with care if we build them with it.

As I took more rides, my fear disappeared. I began to greet the car silently, as though it were an old friend. I found peace in its stillness. I realised that the car, though without a soul, mirrored the discipline and patience of its makers. It reflected human potential — what we can create when we mix imagination with respect for life.

I thought about my people. What would they say if I told them of this? They might laugh, they might not believe. But I would tell them that this car taught me about humility and observation. That the world is moving, and that we must move too — not by abandoning who we are, but by learning how to walk with new things the way we walk with land and weather.

Sometimes, when the car stopped at my destination, I would rest my hand on its cool surface and whisper thank you. It was not just gratitude for the safe ride — it was thanks for the insight, for the calm, for the reminder that courage sometimes means letting go.

By the tenth ride, I no longer watched every move in fear. Instead, I watched the people outside — how they crossed, how they reacted. Some stared with wide eyes; some ignored it completely. Children pointed and laughed. I could see how quickly humans adapt, how curiosity becomes normalcy. It made me think of my own transformation. The first time, I was afraid. Now, I was curious. Now, I was reflective.

Each journey became a mirror. The car's patience showed me my own restlessness. Its precision revealed my clumsiness. Its calm made me aware of my anxiety. And slowly, I began to change. I breathed deeper, observed longer, reacted slower. I began to practice this awareness not only on the road, but in life — in conversations, in study, in thought.

I imagined what would happen if such technology reached my home. If villages could use the same intelligence to predict floods, guide farmers, deliver medicine. If we could blend human wisdom and machine foresight. I saw a future where technology does not replace us but strengthens our ways of knowing — where data meets tradition, and progress walks hand in hand with patience.

Sometimes at night, after my rides, I would sit by my window and watch the lights of the city flicker. I would think about how human beings, in their search for control, had created something that taught surrender. This driverless taxi — built from code, wires, and thought — had reminded me of something ancient: that true wisdom lies in observing, adapting, and moving with grace through the unpredictable.

On my last ride, the city was quiet, wrapped in soft fog. The roads glistened, the world felt hushed. As the car carried me home, I realised I was no longer a passenger of fear but of understanding. I had learned to see beyond the mechanics into the spirit of creation itself. When the car stopped, I sat still for a moment, not wanting to move. Then I touched the dashboard gently, whispered another thank you, and stepped out into the mist.

The street smelled of rain. My reflection glimmered in a puddle beside the car, mixed with the shimmer of neon lights. I walked slowly back to my room, each step light, thoughtful. My mind was full of memories — of mountains, of rivers, of this city of machines and light. I carried them all together, like threads woven into one bilum.

That night, I wrote in my notebook. I wrote that courage is not only in facing danger, but in trusting the unknown. I wrote that patience is not stillness, but readiness. I wrote that the future, like a driverless car, will move whether we are ready or not — and that our task is to move with it, with eyes open, hearts steady, and roots still deep in the soil of who we are.

The driverless taxi did not just carry me across Wuhan. It carried me across my own fear, my own assumptions. It showed me that the future is not something to be afraid of, but something to listen to, like a new song sung in a language you are just beginning to understand.

And so I keep that memory close, like the feel of my bilum on my shoulder — a quiet reminder that even far from home, I can still learn, still trust, still move with the world as it changes.

8

MOVING TO TIANJIN

When my time in Wuhan came to an end, I stood at the railway station with my luggage by my side, the heavy air of central China pressing against my skin, and I felt a mix of excitement and sorrow that is difficult to explain in words. Wuhan had become more than a city to me. It was where I had stumbled through the first strange sounds of Mandarin, where I had burned my tongue on bowls of hot dry noodles and laughed with classmates who barely understood my English, where I had cried in my dormitory when homesickness clutched me like a vine.

It was where I had been tested and where I had grown. Yet, as with the sweet potato harvest in Hela, one must always move from planting ground to new planting ground, because a single garden cannot feed you forever. My scholarship letter had arrived, telling me that the next garden for my mind was in Tianjin University of Technology and Education.

The train ride northward from Wuhan was long, and as I watched the landscapes pass by, I thought about the path my life had already carved. From the ridges of Hela where we Huli women wake before dawn to tend our kaukau mounds, to the crowded lecture halls of UPNG in Port Moresby, to the shining riverbanks of Wuhan, I had walked a road my grandmothers could never have imagined. I pressed my forehead to the glass as villages, fields, and factories streamed past, and I thought of my mother back home, her hands always dark with garden soil, her laughter loud even when the work was hard. I carried her voice inside me, telling me to endure, to keep moving, to remember that a Huli woman's strength is not in loud declarations but in steady perseverance.

When the train finally slowed into Tianjin, I stepped onto the platform and felt the northern air against my face. It was cooler than Wuhan, drier, with a hint of the sea in it.

Wuhan had wrapped itself around me with its river humidity, but Tianjin greeted me differently—its air sharper, its sky broader.

As I looked around at the enormous station, filled with rushing crowds, bright signs, and uniformed officers, I knew this was another kind of China altogether. I was not frightened, but I felt small, as though the city was measuring me and asking silently: Will you manage here?

The taxi ride from the station to the university revealed a city of contradictions that fascinated me from the very first moment. I saw boulevards lined with European-style buildings that looked like they had been transported from another continent, their facades heavy with stone and archways, windows tall and elegant. Then, only a few streets later, I would see traditional Chinese neighborhoods with narrow alleys, red lanterns swaying above doorways, and the smell of dumplings steaming from shops. This mixture confused and thrilled me. In Hela, our houses are round, low, and built from bush materials, every village carrying the same signature of our people. Here, history had left layers of different identities, and Tianjin seemed to embrace them all.

When I finally entered the gates of Tianjin University of Technology and Education, I felt once more that nervous excitement of starting afresh. The university grounds stretched wide, with towering dormitories, classroom blocks, canteens buzzing with life, and banners written in Mandarin characters that I could only partially understand.

I dragged my suitcase along the path and thought, this will be my new garden, my new and much bigger wig school. In Hela, the wig school is where young men go to discipline themselves, to grow their hair into the famous Huli wigs, and to learn patience, sacrifice, and strength. For me, Tianjin would become my wig school of the mind.

From the first day of classes, I realised that my time in Wuhan had been only the beginning. There, my main struggle had been language, and though I had made progress, Tianjin demanded more. The lectures were not language classes anymore—they were about education itself, pedagogy, psychology, curriculum design, all taught in Mandarin. It was as though I had been learning how to paddle a canoe in Wuhan, only to be thrown into the middle of a wide river in Tianjin and told to navigate it. I sat in those lecture halls with my notebook open, straining my ears to catch every phrase, writing down words I did not understand, my mind both exhausted and exhilarated.

Sometimes, in the evenings after a long day of lectures, I would sit in my dormitory room and think about the classrooms back home in Papua New Guinea. I thought of the little wooden desks in rural schools, sometimes three children crowded into one, sharing a single textbook. I thought of the blackboards patched with cracks, of teachers improvising lessons when materials were scarce. I thought of the children's faces, bright with eagerness, even when they had walked hours to get to school.

And then I would compare these images with what I saw in Tianjin: classrooms with projectors, computers, endless stacks of textbooks, students carrying sleek laptops. The contrast was stark, and it stirred something in me— a determination that I must take what I learned here and somehow use it to feed the hunger for knowledge in my homeland.

The people of Tianjin fascinated me just as much as the city. My classmates were diligent, quiet, and respectful, often more reserved than I was used to. In Hela, conversation flows easily; we laugh loudly, we interrupt, we argue and debate in heated bursts. In Tianjin's classrooms, students listened intently, taking notes, rarely speaking unless asked. At first, I felt out of place, my instinct to jump into discussions marking me as different. But slowly, I learned to adapt, to listen more deeply before I spoke, to value silence as much as speech. And in doing so, I gained a new kind of discipline—the ability to let my thoughts ripen before releasing them.

Language remained my greatest challenge. Though my Mandarin had improved in Wuhan, Tianjin introduced me to faster, sharper speech. Locals spoke in tones that sometimes melted together in my ears, and I would stand lost in a crowd, trying to catch the meaning. I remember one particular day in the campus canteen when I tried to order food. I had rehearsed the words in my head as I stood in line, whispering them to myself like a child practicing a song. But when it came my turn, the words tangled on my tongue, and the woman behind the counter frowned, shaking her head. A line of impatient students formed behind me, and I felt the hot flush of shame rise up my neck. Finally, a classmate stepped forward, repeated my order correctly, and the woman handed me my tray.

That night, I sat on my bed, tears prickling my eyes, wondering why I had come so far from home only to stumble on simple things like food. Yet even in that pain, I remembered: patience is the path, for a pig needs many days to grow, just as a man needs many seasons to grow wise. I told myself that every humiliation was part of the fattening, part of the slow process of growing strong.

Winter in Tianjin was another test I had not expected to be so harsh. In Hela, the nights can be cold, especially in the highlands, but there is always the fire, the warmth of the hearth, the laughter of family around the flames. In Tianjin, the cold was a different creature. The wind sliced through my jacket as I walked across campus, my breath clouding the air, my fingers numbing even inside gloves. I longed for the smoky comfort of a Huli house, the sound of pigs snuffling in their pens, the way the firelight flickered against the clay walls. Many nights, as the wind rattled the windows of my dormitory, I closed my eyes and imagined myself back home, crouched by the fire, the warmth seeping into my bones. Those memories became my invisible blanket, carrying me through the freezing days.

Despite these hardships, there were also triumphs that shone brightly. The first time I delivered a presentation in Mandarin and saw my classmates nodding in understanding, I felt a rush of pride unlike anything before. Each exam I passed felt like a mountain climbed, each conversation successfully held in Mandarin a victory carved out of struggle. I began to realise that resilience is not only about surviving hardship but also about celebrating the small steps of progress.

Outside the classroom, I explored Tianjin's streets and markets, eager to immerse myself in its life. I tasted goubuli baozi, the famous steamed buns of Tianjin, their soft dough yielding to flavourful fillings that warmed me against the cold. I walked along the Haihe River at night, watching the city's lights ripple across the water, thinking of the Tagali River back in Hela and how different yet how similar rivers are in carrying the lives of people. I joined local families on evening strolls, listening to the chatter of children, the rhythmic sound of elders practicing tai chi. Slowly, I felt the city opening its arms to me, not as a stranger but as a guest learning its ways.

Through it all, I carried the spirit of my Huli heritage. I thought often of the wigmen schools back home, where young men separate themselves from their families to grow their wigs and discipline their bodies and minds. My time in Tianjin felt like such a school.

I was far from home, living under strict routines, enduring hardships that tested me daily. My wig was not of hair but of knowledge, woven strand by strand through long nights of study, through moments of failure and triumph. And when I finally began to feel confident in my Mandarin, when I found myself not only surviving but thriving in my studies, I knew that my wig had grown, shining with the strength of resilience.

I also thought often of the women of Hela—my mother, my aunts, my sisters—who carried bilums heavy with kaukau, who planted gardens in rocky soil, who endured rain and sun without complaint. Their resilience was my inheritance. Each time I felt close to giving up in Tianjin, I remembered them, and I told myself that if they could carry their loads up the steep ridges of Hela, then I too could carry my load of books and exams across the wide plains of China. The woman who carries the heavy bilum today will walk taller tomorrow. This saying became my anchor, reminding me that my burdens were shaping me, preparing me for the path ahead.

By the time my years in Tianjin drew to a close, I looked back and saw not just struggle but transformation. I had entered the city uncertain, my Mandarin halting, my confidence fragile. I left with a degree in Education, a deeper understanding of discipline, and a heart that had been carved stronger by every challenge. I left knowing that my time in Tianjin had not only trained me academically but had reshaped me as a person. The cold winters, the humiliations in the canteen, the long nights of study—all of them had been my teachers.

And so, when I boarded the train once more, this time leaving Tianjin behind, I carried with me not just the memories of architecture and food, but the invisible wig I had grown—the crown of resilience, discipline, and hope that would stay with me forever.

9

A JOURNEY TO LANZHOU - CHINA'S LESS DEVELOPED HEART

When people speak of China, they usually speak of its shining faces: Shanghai with its glass towers, Beijing with its ancient palaces and political weight, Shenzhen with its technology and speed. Even Wuhan, where I had studied and lived, had become famous far beyond China's borders. But there is another China, one that rarely appears on postcards or news headlines, one that breathes quietly in its mountains and valleys. I discovered this China in Lanzhou, a city that seemed, at first, smaller, rougher, less polished — and yet, in its imperfection, it spoke to me with a voice more familiar than all the shining cities combined.

I went to Lanzhou not because it was celebrated, but because it was not. Something inside me wanted to see beyond the gloss. I had already witnessed the future in Wuhan's skytrains, in Beijing's high-speed rails, in the driverless cars that had once frightened and amazed me. Now I wanted to look backward and sideways, to touch the edges of a China that still carried its own scars, its slower rhythm, its unpolished stones.

The journey itself became my first meditation. I boarded the train in Wuhan, and as it moved across thousands of kilometers, the landscape unfolded like a scroll. First the lush greens of central China, then the rising mountains, the drier slopes, the earth-coloured ridges. The air grew thinner, sharper. Looking out, I felt both distance and closeness: distance because this was another world from Hela, yet closeness because the mountains of Gansu echoed the bones of my own land. They were shaped differently, carved by different winds, but their presence stirred something in me.

As I gazed at the ridges, I asked myself: *Why do mountains call to me no matter where I am?* **Perhaps because** mountains, more than cities, remind us of time. Skyscrapers are built and demolished within decades, but mountains watch centuries pass like clouds. Lanzhou was a city cradled by mountains, just as Tari is. And in that geography, I felt a connection deeper than politics, deeper than economics — a reminder that the human story is always written between the stubborn strength of stone and the flowing persistence of rivers.

When I arrived in Lanzhou, I breathed air that was different from Wuhan's. It was dry, crisp, filled with dust and history. The Yellow River cut through the city, wide and brown, restless in its current. I stood on a bridge one evening, watching the river churn beneath me. The people of Lanzhou call it their lifeline. They speak of it with respect, sometimes even fear. I thought of our rivers in PNG — the Purari, the Fly, the Sepik — also lifelines, also feared, also shaping lives more than governments do.

As I leaned on the bridge, I asked myself: *What does a river mean to a city?* To Lanzhou, the Yellow River was not just water. It was memory. It was the Silk Road. It was famine and survival. It was the endless reminder that all civilisation begins not with towers or machines, but with water that refuses to stop flowing. And then I thought of PNG again. We, too, are a people of rivers and mountains. Yet we sometimes forget that true wealth is not in the mines we dig, but in the waters that feed us, the ridges that hold us, the land that will outlive us.

Lanzhou University became my next teacher. Compared to Wuhan University or Peking University, it did not sparkle.

Its buildings were older, its paint faded, its equipment less impressive. Yet as I walked its campus, I felt an honesty in its simplicity. There was no attempt to dazzle. There was instead a quiet, steady pulse of learning. Students walked quickly, holding books close, their faces marked by determination.

One student I met told me, "We are far from Beijing, but knowledge reaches us too. We just have to work harder to catch it." His words struck me. In them, I heard the voice of every student in PNG who struggles with poor libraries, slow internet, broken classrooms — yet still dreams.

Lanzhou University, in its modesty, became a mirror of what PNG's universities could be: not rich, but alive with hunger.

That night, I could not sleep. I kept thinking: *Does greatness come from shiny buildings, or from hungry hearts?* In Wuhan, I had sometimes felt drowned in abundance — too many books, too many machines, too many opportunities. In Lanzhou, the scarcity sharpened focus. It whispered to me that limitation itself can become a kind of gift, if it pushes us to climb higher. I thought of the students back home who walk for hours to attend classes, who study by kerosene light, who share one textbook among five friends. Are they not, too, carrying this same spirit?

Food became another meditation. Lanzhou's hand-pulled noodles are famous across China. Watching the noodle maker stretch and slap the dough, pulling it into strands with practiced rhythm, I saw more than cooking. I saw patience, tradition, and the quiet dignity of skill passed down by hand. Each bowl of noodles carried history — the Silk Road, the mixing of cultures, the art of surviving with flour and water.

As I ate, I thought of my mother making mumu in Hela, of her hands moving with the same inherited wisdom. I realised: food is more than sustenance. It is memory shaped into taste. Eating Lanzhou noodles was, for me, not just trying a dish. It was tasting the resilience of a people who had known hardship and found beauty in it. I asked myself: What would a foreigner taste if they ate kaukau roasted in Hela soil? Would they, too, feel our story?

The city itself carried its imperfections openly. Its markets were noisy, its walls carried the wear of years, its roads sometimes narrow and crowded. Compared to Shanghai's gloss, Lanzhou felt rough. Yet in that roughness, I found honesty. I walked through alleys where children played with sticks, where women bargained over vegetables, where old men sat smoking in silence. It did not feel poor in spirit. It felt alive.

I thought: *Is perfection always desirable?* Sometimes, when we chase only the image of modernity, we forget the warmth of imperfection. Lanzhou reminded me that a city does not need to shine to be alive. And PNG, with all its struggles, with its dust and noise and laughter, is alive in the same way. Perhaps our task is not to erase imperfection, but to let it coexist with progress, to allow beauty to emerge even from the cracks.

The provincial museum deepened my reflections. Inside, I saw relics of the Silk Road: coins, maps, pieces of silk. Lanzhou had once been a passage, a place where cultures met and exchanged. It had never been the richest, but it had been essential. Standing there, I asked myself: *What is PNG's role in the world?* We may never be the richest nation, but can we be a bridge? Between the Pacific and Asia, between old wisdom and new knowledge, between tradition and technology? Lanzhou's history whispered yes.

Each day in Lanzhou became a dialogue between past and future, between China and PNG, between what is and what could be. And each dialogue reshaped me.

On my last evening, I returned to the Yellow River. The sun was setting, painting the water gold. I leaned on the railing and felt the wind on my face. I thought of my people back home, sitting by the fire, telling stories under the stars. I thought of the students in Lanzhou, walking quickly with their books. I thought of myself, caught between two worlds, trying to weave them together.

And then it came to me: Lanzhou was not just a city. It was a lesson carved in dust and water. It told me that development is uneven, but not hopeless. That imperfection can carry beauty. That history is not dead, but a living river. That knowledge does not need glass towers; it needs hunger.

I whispered to the river that night: *I will carry this lesson home.* **Because PNG needs to know what I learned in Lanzhou** — that our struggles are not a sentence, but a stage. That our rivers and mountains are not obstacles, but lifelines. That our imperfections are not shame, but starting points. If Lanzhou could rise, so can we.

As the train carried me back to Wuhan, I felt quiet inside. Lanzhou had not dazzled me with towers. It had not overwhelmed me with speed. Instead, it had given me something more enduring: perspective. And sometimes, perspective is the deepest gift a journey can give.

I closed my eyes and saw two rivers flowing side by side — the Yellow River of Lanzhou and the rivers of Hela. Both carried stories, both carried struggles, both carried hope. And I knew then, with a certainty as deep as the mountains, that my journey between worlds was not just about seeing difference, but about recognising the same heartbeat beneath it all.

10

XIAOBEI NIGHT MARKET - A LITTLE AFRICA IN CHINA

When I first heard of Xiaobei, people called it "Little Africa in China." The words stirred my imagination long before my feet touched its streets. I had already walked through Shanghai's glittering towers, I had wandered among Wuhan's lakes, I had stood at the edges of the Yellow River in Lanzhou. But Xiaobei was something different. It was not only Chinese. It was a crossing place; a knot tied with many threads. And when I finally walked there, on a humid evening, my heart felt both curious and unsettled — as if I was about to step into another world hidden inside China.

I arrived by metro. As the train doors opened, the air itself seemed to shift. There was more noise, more smell, more colour. I followed the flow of people out of the station and into the narrow streets. Neon lights flickered. Music floated from tiny shops — sometimes reggae, sometimes Afrobeat, sometimes Arabic rhythms. The smell of roasted meat, of spices heavy with cumin and chili, of fried plantains, filled my nose. I had entered Xiaobei Night Market.

At first, I simply stood still, letting the place wash over me. Africans moved in groups, laughing, bargaining, carrying bags of goods. Chinese vendors called out prices in Mandarin. A group of Middle Eastern men leaned by a stall, smoking and speaking fast Arabic. It was noisy, messy, alive. I felt as if the world itself had squeezed into one narrow street.

As I walked deeper, I saw stalls selling clothes — bright fabrics from West Africa, patterned dresses, headscarves, leather shoes polished to shine. The colours reminded me of Hagen market back home, where women sell meri blouses in long lines, each fabric shouting its own design. In Xiaobei, too, clothes were more than cloth. They were identities hung in the open.

I passed a food stall where skewers of lamb sizzled over hot coals. The vendor brushed them with oil and spice, the smell rising like a song. I stopped and asked for two skewers. When I bit into the first, the flavour burst — hot, smoky, tender. The man beside me, a tall Nigerian, grinned and said, "Good, eh?" I nodded, unable to speak because my mouth was already burning. We both laughed, two strangers joined by spice.

That laughter broke my hesitation. I realised Xiaobei was not a place to stand on the side. It was a place to enter, to taste, to talk. So, I walked further, touching fabrics, sniffing spices, letting my ears drink the languages swirling around me. English mixed with French, French with Chinese, Chinese with Lingala. It was a storm of voices, and somehow I loved being lost in it.

One corner of the market was filled with food from Africa. There were piles of yams, bunches of plantains, bags of cassava flour. My eyes widened when I saw sweet potatoes stacked in a basket. They were longer than the kaukau from Hela, but their presence pulled my heart home. I thought of my mother peeling kaukau for mumu, of children eating roasted sweet potatoes by the roadside. I touched one gently, almost wanting to take it back to PNG as proof that food travels just as people do.

At a small restaurant with a faded sign reading "Mama Africa," I decided to sit and eat. Inside, the walls were painted with murals of African landscapes — lions, elephants, wide savannahs under red sunsets. The smell of pepper soup filled the air. I ordered jollof rice because I had heard of it but never tasted it. When the plate arrived, the rice was red with tomato and spice, topped with fried chicken. The first mouthful shocked me. It was both strange and familiar — the heat of the chili, the comfort of rice, the sharpness of tomato. My mind leapt home again, to PNG's chicken curry shared at celebrations. Different, yes, but carrying the same soul: food as joy, food as togetherness.

While I ate, I struck up a conversation with a young woman from Ghana who sat at the next table. She was a student, like me, studying business in Guangzhou. "Xiaobei is where we come when we miss home," she told me. "We find our food here, our people here. It is not Ghana, but it helps."

Her words touched me. I thought of how I sometimes longed for the taste of taro or pitpit, how I carried dried kaukau in my suitcase when I first came to China. I realised that every migrant carries two hungers — one for the future, one for the taste of home. And markets like Xiaobei feed both.

Later that night, I wandered into a music shop. Drums of all sizes stood stacked, their skins shining under dim light. A young man from Cameroon sat tapping rhythms on one, his hands moving quick and sure. I stood and listened, my body swaying without my permission. The beat reminded me of the kundu drum in Hela, the heartbeat of our *singsings*. Different rhythm, different continent, but the same truth: the drum speaks the language of the body before the mind can catch up.

The Cameroonian noticed me and handed me a small drum. "Try," he said. I hesitated, then tapped slowly, awkwardly. He encouraged me, adding his rhythm until together we made a stumbling but joyful sound. People gathered, clapping, laughing. For a moment, Xiaobei Night Market turned into a festival ground, strangers united by rhythm.

Walking back out into the open air, I thought deeply: Is this not the future of the world? People from far lands, each carrying their own drum, their own spice, their own story — all meeting in one place, clashing and blending until a new song is born?

Xiaobei reminded me of PNG in a strange way. My country is also made of many tribes, many languages, each with its own drum, its own flavour. When we meet, sometimes we clash. But when we learn to blend, when we share food and song, something powerful happens. Perhaps the world is simply a larger PNG, and places like Xiaobei are the *singsing* grounds where global tribes meet.

Of course, not everything in Xiaobei was joyful. I noticed the heavy presence of police, the cautious glances of some vendors. I heard whispers about raids, about visas, about struggles of Africans trying to make a living in China. It reminded me that multiculturalism is not always easy.

Beneath the music and flavour, there were also tensions. I thought of migrants in PNG too — the Chinese shopkeepers in Port Moresby, the Filipinos working in Lae — and the ways my own people sometimes looked at them with suspicion. Diversity brings beauty, but it also demands patience, openness, and trust. Xiaobei showed me both sides: the celebration and the challenge.

When midnight approached, the market did not sleep. In fact, it seemed to wake even more. More lights blinked on, more grills sizzled, more voices rose. I bought a small bag of fried plantains to take back. As I walked, I passed a stall selling second-hand shoes. The vendor, a tall man with dreadlocks, called out, "Sister, good shoes, cheap price!" I laughed and shook my head. He laughed back, undisturbed. The air was full of such exchanges, half-serious, half-playful, yet carrying the warmth of human connection.

Finally, I found a quiet corner and sat with my plantains. Around me, life pulsed, but I felt still. I thought of how far I had come — from the mountains of Hela to this noisy night market in Guangzhou, surrounded by Africans, Arabs, Chinese, and others. I asked myself: What does it mean to belong in a place like this? Perhaps belonging is not always about blood or passport. Perhaps belonging is the courage to sit down, to eat, to laugh, to drum — to make yourself part of the rhythm of a place.

As I ate the sweet plantains, I whispered in my heart: This too is home, even if only for tonight.

And that was the gift of Xiaobei Night Market.

It was not just a place to buy or sell. It was a mirror that showed me the world inside China, and the China inside the world. It reminded me that being a Huli woman in China meant more than learning Mandarin or passing exams. It meant opening my heart to the unexpected, tasting food from Ghana, drumming with a Cameroonian, laughing with a Nigerian, watching Arabic words float in the Guangzhou night.

When I left, the market still glowed behind me, alive as ever. I carried with me the taste of jollof, the beat of drums, the sight of bright fabrics, the smell of cumin. But more than that, I carried a truth: the world is not divided neatly into nations. The world is a night market, messy and noisy, sometimes tense, but full of possibilities when we choose to meet.

And deep inside, I promised myself: one day, when I return to PNG, I will tell my people about Xiaobei. I will tell them that in China's great cities, there is also a little Africa, a place where diversity breathes openly. I will tell them that our future, too, depends on how well we can turn our markets into meeting grounds, our streets into bridges, our differences into songs.

11

DISCOVERING CHINA'S EDUCATION SYSTEM

When I first entered the gates of the Tianjin University of Technology and Education (TUTE), I felt the weight of a journey that began not in China, not even in Port Moresby, but deep in the green valleys of Hela

Province. For me, education was never just about classrooms, books, and exams. It was about survival, memory, and the passing of wisdom through generations.

In Huli culture, children grow up in a world where learning begins with the land. Our textbooks were the ridges of sweet potato mounds. Our blackboards were the bark of trees where elders carved markings to teach us clan boundaries. Our classrooms were smoky huts, where the old men sat by the fire and told stories that wove together history, morality, and identity.

My earliest memory of education was not holding a pencil, but listening. My father and uncles recited genealogies, sometimes for hours. They traced our clan's origin, our land boundaries, the names of ancestors who fought in battles long before I was born. If I drifted into sleep or lost focus, I would be corrected: "A true Huli must know where she comes from. Without memory, you are like a pig wandering in another man's garden."

Those words stayed with me. In our world, knowledge was not optional—it was life itself. Forgetting the boundaries of your clan's land could mean losing your inheritance. Forgetting your ancestors' names could mean shame before the elders. Forgetting the right ritual could anger the spirits. Education, in this sense, was woven into our identity.

When I later entered formal schooling, I carried this Huli training with me. But what I encountered in the classroom in Koroba or later in Port Moresby was very different.

Teachers had chalk, exercise books, and lessons that came from government syllabuses. We were told to memorise dates of independence, formulas for mathematics, and English grammar rules. It was a new system—structured, but also fragile. Resources were scarce. Sometimes we had no textbooks. Sometimes teachers did not arrive. Yet through it all, I carried my Huli discipline: listen carefully, memorise, and be ready to speak with authority when called upon.

That early foundation, both tribal and formal, became the lens through which I later discovered the Chinese education system.

My first year in China, spent in Wuhan for the foundation program, introduced me to the basics of Mandarin and the routines of Chinese campus life. But it was only in Tianjin, at TUTE, that I truly came face to face with the depth and intensity of China's educational culture.

The first difference I noticed was scale. In PNG, my classes in Hela rarely went beyond 30 students. At TUTE, lectures had 55 to 65 students, sometimes more. Yet despite the numbers, the classes ran like clockwork. Students arrived before the lecturer.

Nobody wandered in late. Desks were lined neatly, textbooks open, pens ready.

Discipline was visible in every corner. Before the teacher entered, the room was hushed. When the lecturer greeted us, the students stood in unison. It reminded me of how we Huli people rise to our feet when an elder enters the men's house, lowering our gaze to show respect. In that moment, I realised that though worlds apart, Huli and Chinese traditions both place great value on honouring those who carry knowledge.

The second difference was structure. In PNG, lessons often depended on the creativity of teachers. Some teachers stuck to the textbook; others allowed students to debate and question. At TUTE, the structure was uniform and standardised. Lectures introduced theories, followed by seminars for group discussion. Homework was checked systematically. Essays had clear rubrics. Examinations followed a national schedule. It was as if the entire system had been engineered to run smoothly, like the trains I saw arriving in Tianjin station exactly on time.

One of the greatest challenges I faced was academic writing. In PNG, especially in high school, essays were often descriptive: write about a festival, describe your village, explain a process. At TUTE, essays demanded theory. I had to read education philosophers, interpret their arguments, and defend my own stance. It was no longer about retelling — it was about reasoning.

This reminded me of the Huli men's house debates. When clans disputed land, the men would gather. Each man presented genealogies, tracing boundaries and ancestors to prove ownership. It was never enough to say, "This land is mine." One had to prove it by citing the chain of ancestors who planted, fought, and lived there. Similarly, in TUTE essays, it was not enough to say, "I believe in collaborative learning." I had to cite Vygotsky, compare him to Piaget, and explain why one theory worked better in certain contexts.

Examinations in China also carried enormous weight. In PNG, exams were important, but teachers often balanced them with continuous assessment. At TUTE, exams felt like the final word. Weeks of study led to that one decisive moment. I remember my first education theory exam: 10 essay questions, each demanding precise recall and critical application. The pressure was immense. Yet it taught me endurance—the same endurance I learned as a girl carrying bilums of firewood up Hela's steep hills. The burden feels heavy at first, but each step, each breath, carries you closer to your goal.

What fascinated me most in China was the cohort system. Students entered as a group and stayed together year after year, forming bonds that went beyond friendship. They studied together, ate together, and prepared for exams together. If one student fell behind, the others helped. The success of the individual was tied to the success of the group.

This resonated with my Huli upbringing. In the men's house, boys grew together, learning side by side until they were ready for initiation. No one walked the path alone. If one boy weakened, the group encouraged him. If one forgot a ritual, the others corrected him. Just as the Huli believed in collective strength, the Chinese system embodied the same spirit.

In PNG's modern schools, however, students were reshuffled each year. Bonds were looser. Students competed individually. Seeing the Chinese model, I wondered: what if PNG schools adopted this collective approach? Would more of our struggling students succeed if they felt the weight of the group behind them?

Another striking feature was the practice of looping— teachers moving up with their students year after year. In PNG, teachers usually specialised in one grade. Once you passed, you moved on to someone new. In Hela, however, elders mentored the same boys for years, guiding them until they were ready to stand as men. I saw this same philosophy in China.

My lecturers at TUTE were more than instructors. They became guides. They tracked our progress not just for one semester but across years, noticing our growth, our struggles, our habits. They reminded me of Huli elders who scolded, encouraged, and shaped us patiently.

The continuity built trust. It taught me that education was not only about transferring information, but about building relationships that nurtured the soul.

Respect defined the classroom atmosphere. Students stood to answer questions. Assignments were handed in with both hands. Teachers were addressed with titles like "our dear teacher." At first, this felt rigid. In PNG classrooms, especially in Port Moresby, students often joked with teachers, challenged them openly, and debated freely. But then I remembered my Huli roots.

In the men's house, we never spoke to elders as equals. We lowered our voices. We brought gifts with both hands. We learned by watching first, then speaking carefully. The Chinese discipline was not foreign—it was familiar. It reminded me that respect is not weakness but a form of humility that opens the heart to receive knowledge.

One area where China amazed me was technology. Classrooms had projectors, online learning platforms, and digital resources. Students submitted assignments electronically. Lecturers used PowerPoint slides that were shared in advance. In PNG, especially in Hela, even chalk was sometimes scarce. Here, knowledge flowed through screens, making learning faster and broader.

Yet I also reflected critically. Technology made learning efficient, but sometimes it reduced human interaction. Back home, storytelling required eye contact, gestures, and emotional connection. Would too much reliance on screens weaken the bond between teacher and student? I resolved that when I returned to PNG, I would embrace technology, but never at the cost of the human touch that defined Huli learning.

Despite its strengths, I noticed limitations in the Chinese system. Students avoided political discussions. Essays never questioned government policies. Sensitive topics were off-limits. In PNG, we had more freedom. We could challenge teachers, question leaders, and argue openly as long as we had evidence. The Huli way also valued debate, sometimes fierce, as a tool of truth.

In China, silence on sensitive issues created a gap. Knowledge was vast, but critical freedom was constrained. I admired the order and discipline, but I also longed for the openness of PNG classrooms and Huli debates.

One strength of TUTE was the emphasis on internships. We were encouraged to teach in local schools, applying theories in practice. It reminded me of Huli boys learning to garden or hunt by actually doing it alongside their elders. Theory alone was never enough; practice was essential.

I still remember my first internship in Tianjin. The classroom was large, with 60 students, yet order was maintained. I struggled to give instructions in Mandarin, but the experience taught me resilience. Each mistake became a stepping stone. By the end, I felt the pride of seeing students respond to my guidance. It was like planting kaukau in rocky soil and finally seeing the vines sprout.

Outside the classroom, the environment also shaped my educational journey. In Tianjin, I could walk at night without fear. Libraries stayed open late, giving me a safe space to study. Scholarships made it possible for me to pursue higher learning. I thought of my sisters in Hela, many of whom never had the chance to go beyond primary school because of cost, distance, or safety concerns. China offered what PNG could not: security, affordability, and opportunity.

Yet I never forgot my roots. Each time I succeeded in Tianjin, I felt the invisible presence of my ancestors, the Huli wigmen who endured long years of discipline in wig schools. Just as they grew their wigs strand by strand, I grew my knowledge page by page.

Looking back, I see three systems that shaped me. Huli education taught me respect, memory, and endurance. PNG schooling gave me dialogue, openness, and freedom of expression. Chinese education gave me structure, rigor, and collective responsibility.

Each had strengths, each had weaknesses. Together, they wove the fabric of who I became: a Huli woman, a PNG citizen, and a student shaped by China.

Education, I realised, is not only about passing exams or earning degrees. It is about shaping identity, cultivating resilience, and preparing us to serve our people. From Hela's smoky huts to Tianjin's digital classrooms, my journey showed me that no system is complete on its own. But when woven together, they create something powerful: a vision of learning that honours tradition, embraces freedom, and applies discipline.

One of the ancient proverbs says: the man who carries the heavy bilum today will walk taller tomorrow. In China, I carried the bilum of essays, exams, and theories. It was heavy, but it made me taller—not in height, but in wisdom.

When I return to PNG, I know my task is to carry this wisdom home, to weave the lessons of three worlds into an education system that can uplift our people.

12

EXPERIENCING CHINESE FOOD CULTURE

When I think about my years in China, the first thing that always comes to my mind is food. It is strange how smells and tastes can carry so many memories.

Sometimes when I smell sesame oil, or hear the sound of a wok on high fire, I can almost see the streets, the people, and the faces that were once part of my everyday life.

Chinese food became more than something I ate; it became the way I learned about the country, the people, and even myself. Through every meal, I found stories, friendships, and lessons that still live inside me.

Wuhan was the first city that shaped my understanding of Chinese food culture. The city was full of noise and energy. Early in the morning, the streets came alive with people selling breakfast from small stalls. The air was heavy with the smell of noodles, soy sauce, and chili. Every corner had something to taste, something new to learn. The most famous dish in Wuhan was hot dry noodles, reganmian. I remember the first time I tried them. The noodles were thick, and the sauce was made from sesame paste, chili oil, soy sauce, and garlic. The first bite was strong — spicy, nutty, and rich. It filled my mouth with fire and flavour, and I could not stop eating. I watched people eat it quickly, standing at the side of the road, wiping sweat from their faces but still smiling. That was the moment I realised how deeply food could be part of a place's spirit.

In Wuhan, food was everywhere — in the streets, in tiny restaurants, in night markets that stayed open until midnight. I loved walking through those markets, seeing the bright lights reflecting on wet pavement after rain. Vendors shouted prices, oil sizzled, and steam rose from pots. I tasted grilled skewers, dumplings, and bowls of spicy soup that warmed me from the inside out.

Food in Wuhan was bold and full of life, like the city itself. It taught me that eating was not only about filling your stomach; it was about joining the rhythm of the place you live in.

After a year, I moved to Tianjin, a city close to the sea. Tianjin felt softer, more peaceful, with wide streets and cool winds. The food there had a gentler flavour but was no less rich in meaning. Mornings in Tianjin always began with the smell of steamed buns — **baozi** — sold on almost every street corner. I would stand in line, watching the steam rise from bamboo baskets, and when I bit into one, the warm filling spread across my tongue. Sometimes it was pork and cabbage, sometimes vegetables or sweet red bean. Each bun was simple but comforting, like a small piece of kindness to start the day.

There was an old woman who lived near my apartment. Everyone called her Grandma Li. She often sat outside her house, peeling vegetables or chatting with neighbours. One day, when she saw me returning from the market with dumpling wrappers, she called me over and asked if I knew how to make dumplings. I told her I was still learning. She laughed softly and invited me into her kitchen. It was a small space, but it smelled wonderful — a mix of ginger, garlic, and soy sauce. She showed me how to make dumplings properly. We rolled out the dough, placed the filling in the center, and folded it into small half-moons. My first few were messy, and she teased me kindly, but by the end, they began to look better.

We boiled them and waited for the water to bubble. When the dumplings floated to the top, she scooped them out, and we dipped them in vinegar and chili oil. As I ate, she told me about her childhood, about how dumplings were a symbol of reunion in Chinese families, especially during the New Year. I listened quietly, touched by how much meaning could hide inside a simple dish. Since then, dumplings have never been just food to me; they became a reminder of warmth, patience, and the beauty of shared moments.

Tianjin was also where I discovered jianbing, a kind of breakfast pancake. Every morning, I watched the street vendor make it — fast and skillful. He spread a thin layer of batter on a round hot plate, cracked an egg on top, added onions, sauce, and a piece of crispy dough, then folded it up neatly. It took less than a minute. The sound of the metal spatula against the hot surface became part of my morning routine. I would eat it as I walked to class, the sauce dripping slightly on my fingers, but I didn't mind. Food in Tianjin taught me about balance — between sweet and salty, soft and crispy, simplicity and skill.

Later, life took me to Beijing. The capital was big, full of history, and full of people from every corner of China. Food in Beijing was like a museum of flavours — traditional and modern, simple and luxurious, all mixed together. One of my first memories there was eating Peking duck. A friend invited me to a restaurant famous for it. The chef brought the whole roasted duck to the table and sliced it thinly with quick, sharp cuts. The skin was golden and crisp. We wrapped the slices in small pancakes with cucumber, green onion, and sweet bean sauce. The combination of flavours — the salt of the duck, the freshness of the cucumber, the sweetness of the sauce — felt perfect. I remember thinking that this dish carried hundreds of years of history, passed from emperors to ordinary people.

Beijing winters were cold, and during those months, hotpot became my favorite. A pot of boiling soup sat in the center of the table, and everyone cooked their own food in it — thin slices of meat, mushrooms, tofu, greens, and noodles. The bubbling sound, the rising steam, and the laughter around the table made the cold outside disappear. Eating hotpot was an experience of togetherness. It wasn't only about the food but the sharing — dipping your chopsticks into the same pot, waiting together, talking, and laughing. It felt like family even when we were just friends. That sense of closeness taught me something deep about Chinese culture: food is the language of care.

One of the most meaningful food experiences I ever had in China happened when a friend invited me to her village, far from the busy streets of the city. Her parents welcomed me warmly, and when it was time to eat, they served a table full of dishes — vegetables, fish, meat, and rice — all carefully cooked and full of colour. The food looked beautiful, and the smell made me hungry at once. I ate slowly, enjoying each dish, but when I couldn't finish everything on my plate, I tried to set it aside. My friend smiled gently and told me to finish my food. She said that in her family, it was a sin to throw away food.

Later that evening, she told me why. During the war between the Japanese soldiers and the Chinese people, her parents and grandparents had gone without food for months. They had to eat whatever they could find — things that growled, swam, and flew — just to survive. Since then, her family had made a promise never to waste even a single grain of rice. Every meal was treated with respect because it reminded them of how hard life once was.

That story stayed with me deeply. I learned to keep leftovers warm for the next day and eat them gratefully, the way they did. I also noticed how much patience they had when cooking. They never made just one dish; they always prepared several, each with its own flavour and colour. Every dish took time, and they cooked it with care and attention. Watching them, I realised that Chinese people cook not just for eating but for sharing love.

I thought of how, back home in Hela, we often cook everything in one pot — meat, vegetables, everything together. It fills the stomach, but it shows how impatient we can be. In China, I saw that cooking was an act of patience, an expression of respect for each ingredient. That lesson changed how I thought about food and about people. It taught me that good food requires time, effort, and heart.

Beijing also showed me how food follows the seasons. In summer, people ate cold noodles, light and refreshing. In autumn, there were mooncakes for the Mid-Autumn Festival, filled with lotus seed paste or red beans. In winter, hot soups and dumplings kept everyone warm. Each season had its own colours, flavours, and traditions. I began to understand how food and time were connected — how people used food to celebrate change and to remember the past.

After some years, I moved again, this time to Shanghai. Shanghai felt different — modern, bright, fast. The lights reflected on the river at night, and the streets never seemed to sleep. The food there was also full of energy. People in Shanghai liked dishes that were delicate, slightly sweet, and beautifully presented. I quickly fell in love with xiao long bao, small soup dumplings. The first time I ate one, I didn't know the proper way. I bit too hard, and the hot soup spilled out, burning my tongue. My friends laughed and taught me to bite a small hole first, sip the soup, and then eat the dumpling. From then on, it became a small pleasure I never tired of.

Shanghai mornings often began with shengjian bao, pan-fried buns with crispy bottoms and soft tops. There was a small shop near my building that sold them. The lady who worked there always greeted me with a big smile and a few friendly words.

I liked to watch her cook. She moved with confidence, turning the buns in the pan, letting them turn golden before adding a bit of water and covering the lid. When she lifted the lid, the sound of sizzling filled the air, and steam wrapped around us. I took my breakfast to go, walking down the busy street with the smell of fried dough following me. Those small moments made my days bright.

Living in Shanghai also encouraged me to cook more for myself. I visited wet markets, where vendors sold fresh vegetables, fish, and spices. I learned which soy sauces were light and which were dark, how to use rice vinegar, and how to balance salt and sugar in stir-fried dishes. I began experimenting — mixing flavours I learned in other cities, creating new ones. Sometimes my dishes turned out perfectly; sometimes they didn't. But I loved the process. Cooking became a form of meditation, a quiet way to feel connected to all the people who had taught me through their food.

Through all these years, I came to see that Chinese food culture is not only about what people eat, but how they eat. Meals are meant to be shared. Dishes are placed in the center of the table, and everyone takes a little of each. No one eats alone. There is always conversation, laughter, and the clinking of chopsticks. Even simple meals have meaning — they show respect, generosity, and care. I learned that when someone offers you food, it is a way of saying, "You belong here."

Festivals made this meaning even stronger. During the Dragon Boat Festival, I joined friends to make zongzi — sticky rice dumplings wrapped in bamboo leaves. The process was slow and careful. We filled the leaves with rice, beans, and meat, folded them tightly, and tied them with string. When they were steamed, the smell filled the whole house. During the Mid-Autumn Festival, we shared mooncakes and tea, watching the full moon together. Each festival came with its own taste, and each taste carried stories of ancestors, legends, and blessings for the future.

As time passed, Chinese food became part of who I was. The rhythm of meals, the meaning behind sharing, the attention to balance — all these shaped the way I saw the world. I learned that food is never just food. It is history, memory, and emotion. It is a way of understanding people, of showing kindness, of feeling at home even far from where you started.

When I walk through my memories now, they come back as flavours and scents. I see Wuhan in a bowl of noodles, Tianjin in a steamed bun, Beijing in a crispy piece of duck, and Shanghai in a soup dumpling. Each city gave me a different taste, a different lesson. Wuhan taught me courage and curiosity — the boldness of spice and heat. Tianjin gave me comfort — the soft, gentle warmth of homemade food. Beijing taught me tradition — the power of flavours that survive through time. Shanghai gave me creativity — the beauty of mixing old and new. Together, they formed a journey of taste and life.

Sometimes, even now, I close my eyes and imagine myself walking through a Chinese market again. The air is full of voices, colours, and smells. There are baskets of garlic, piles of ginger, bright green vegetables, and shiny red chilies. The sound of oil sizzling in a pan mixes with laughter and the hum of people talking. I feel at home there — surrounded by life, by flavour, by the shared joy of food.

All these years of living and eating in China have taught me something that goes beyond cooking or recipes.

Food is about connection.

It is about sitting together and saying, "Let's share what we have." It is about respect — for the ingredients, for the people, for the moment. It is about balance — between flavours, between people, between the past and the present. Chinese food culture carries all these lessons quietly, like the aroma that fills a kitchen.

Even after so many meals, I still find joy in the smallest things — the smell of freshly cooked rice, the sound of chopsticks tapping a bowl, the warmth of soup on a cold day. Every dish reminds me of the people I met, the laughter we shared, and the understanding that grew between us. I think that is what food is meant to do — to remind us that no matter where we are, we can find belonging in the simple act of eating together.

When I think of my time in China now, I do not count the years or the places. I count the meals. I count the friendships built around tables, the smiles exchanged over bowls of noodles, the quiet gratitude that comes from sharing food with others. Those moments are the true flavour of my life in China — warm, human, and full of heart.

13

FIFTEEN FACES OF CHINA: A JOURNEY ACROSS THE NATION

When I was a small girl in the Koroba Valley, the mountains were the edge of everything I knew. They stood tall, like guardians, holding the world inside their arms. Mist rolled down from their ridges each evening, wrapping trees in its soft cloak. To me, beyond that mist lay nothing—no people, no rivers, no villages. Only the sky.

My father painted his face yellow and red with earth from our garden. I remember watching him kneel by the fire, dipping his fingers into clay and smearing it across his cheeks. He told me, "These colours come from the land. They give me strength." My mother sat behind me, plaiting my hair, humming soft songs of ancestors. She told me, "Our people walked this land before us. Their spirits are still here." Her hands pulled gently on my hair, steady and patient.

Our lives were measured by pigs, by gardens, by the shifting friendships and rivalries of kin. Some days, my brothers chased pigs through the gardens. Other days, we sat listening to elders telling stories of war and peace, of ghosts in the forest. I believed them all. At night, the flames from the fire painted shadows on the walls of our house, and those shadows became spirits in my young mind.

I never dreamed of airplanes. I never imagined metal birds carrying people into the sky. I thought the valley was all there was.

But life surprises us. Years later, I stood in Port Moresby with a passport in my hand. My heart beat so fast I thought it might break. I was about to leave Papua New Guinea for the first time. I was going to China.

The airplane shook as it prepared to fly. I clutched the seat, whispering a prayer to the ancestors: "Carry me safely." When the engines roared, I felt as if the ground pulled at my stomach while the sky pulled at my head. My ears popped, my eyes widened, and suddenly the world below became small. Rivers looked like silver threads. Mountains looked like wrinkles on a sleeping mat. Clouds swallowed us, and I pressed my face to the window, in awe and fear.

Airports were another kind of world. So many people moved quickly, signs hung everywhere, and voices came through loudspeakers I could not understand. I felt like a child again, lost in a forest of strangers. But soon I was seated again in the silver bird, heading north to a land bigger than my imagination.

Beijing was the first face of China.

The city spread wide and proud, like a chief arriving at a *singsing*. The streets were broader than rivers, and cars flowed like water in all directions. Buildings rose into the sky like glass mountains. People filled every corner, rushing, shouting, carrying bags, their footsteps a steady thunder. I felt small and invisible. In my valley, ten people make a crowd. In Beijing, thousands pressed around me.

At first, I was afraid. But then the smells of food pulled me in. Pots clattered. Voices bargained. Smoke rose from stalls. It felt like home—like Tari market, only much bigger. Instead of kaukau and bananas, there were dumplings, buns soft like pillows, ducks roasted golden, and noodles pulled long like ropes.

One vendor handed me a dumpling. I bit into it, and hot broth spilled over my tongue. I gasped, then laughed. Food could hide a secret! It was as if the dumpling had played a trick on me. The vendor laughed too, clapping his hands. In that moment, I felt the first thread of connection between my valley and this vast city.

I walked through the Forbidden City, past walls that once guarded emperors. The courtyards stretched endlessly, filled with red pillars and golden roofs. I thought of our big-men in Koroba. They had no walls, no armies. Their power came from pigs, words, and their reputations. Yet the weight they carried for their people was the same as the emperors'. Leadership, I realised, has many faces but one heart.

That night, I lay in bed, unable to sleep. Outside, cars honked and engines roared. It sounded like restless spirits running. I thought of home, where the night was filled with frogs singing, dogs barking, and drums beating softly. I missed that rhythm, but I also felt excited—China was only beginning to show me its faces.

Shanghai was the second face.

If Beijing was a chief, old and dignified, Shanghai was youth—restless, ambitious, full of fire.

The city glittered with towers of glass. At night, neon lights painted the river in dazzling colours. Standing at the Bund, I saw two sides of Shanghai. On one side, the Bund's old stone buildings stood firm and heavy, a reminder of history. On the other, Pudong's towers shimmered, rising like dreams into the night sky. Two faces gazing at each other across the river, past and future speaking silently together.

I walked among women my age. They wore silk dresses, their hair shiny, their hands holding glowing screens. They asked me about my home. I told them of pig exchanges, of wigs made from human hair, of gardens where women sang as they worked. They stared at me, their mouths open in wonder. In return, I listened to their stories of elevators, subways that ran under the ground, and offices in towers that touched the sky. We laughed together at our differences, but underneath I felt the closeness of woman-to-woman exchanges. Whether in Shanghai or Koroba, we all carry hopes, dreams, and burdens.

One evening, I watched a cook pull noodles by hand. He stretched the dough again and again, twisting it, folding it, until thin strands filled his hands. I thought of my mother in our garden, stretching kaukau vines as she planted them. Both acts were rhythms of care, both fed families.

In Shanghai, I tasted the future. It dazzled, but it also made me wonder: what does progress mean, and what do we lose when we climb too fast?

From Shanghai, I travelled north to Tianjin, a city by the sea.

Tianjin carried a different air. Its streets were wide and orderly, lined with European-style houses, their walls pale and strong. They looked strange to me, as if they belonged to another land but had planted themselves here. History had left its mark—foreign powers once claimed pieces of this city.

I thought of my own valley. Foreigners had come there too, bringing steel, guns, and new gods. They left changes behind, some good, some heavy. I realised then that every land wears the scars of outsiders. Some scars fade. Some remain sharp.

But Tianjin was not only about the past. Life here was full of joy. Children chased pigeons in the open squares, their laughter rising like the birds themselves. A vendor cooked pancakes hot on a flat pan, cracking an egg inside, sprinkling herbs and chili, folding it quick and neat. He handed it to me wrapped in paper. The taste was warm, rich, and comforting.

Later, I rode a ferris wheel—the biggest I had ever seen. From the top, the city stretched out, streets glowing like threads of fire in the night. Looking down, I saw people as tiny as ants. My heart whispered: From above, all lives are small—whether in a valley or a metropolis.

From Tianjin, I journeyed inland to Hubei.

Hubei's face was drawn by the Yangtze River. When I first saw it, I stopped and stared. It was wider than any river I had known. Back home, rivers rush brown and quick over stones, laughing loudly, filled with spirit voices. The Yangtze was slow and heavy, like an old snake winding across centuries. Its breath was steady, its weight immense.

People spoke of the Three Gorges Dam, a great wall of concrete holding back the river. They said it gave light to millions, but also that it swallowed villages and graves. I wondered if human hands can truly command a river. Our elders always warned us: rivers are alive, and they cannot be tamed without cost.

In Wuhan, I climbed the Yellow Crane Tower. Poets of long ago once stood there, gazing at the river with longing in their eyes. I leaned against the railing, the wind cool on my face, and whispered my own poem:

Carry my voice downstream,

mix it with voices of old,

let it flow to those yet unborn.

I felt the river take my words, just as our own streams at home carry songs when we bathe or wash food. Rivers listen. Rivers remember.

From Hubei, the road carried me further north to Jilin.

Jilin surprised me with snow.

I had never seen snow before. My first step crunched the white powder, and I laughed so hard I clapped my hands. My breath puffed out like smoke, curling in the frozen air. Children around me ran with fireworks and sparklers, their cheeks red, their eyes bright.

It was the Lunar New Year. Every house had red paper pasted on doors. Firecrackers popped like our bamboo cannons at Christmas time, but louder, sharper, filling the night with excitement. The air smelled of gunpowder, smoke, and food.

I joined a family for dinner. They served dumplings, their dough folded in neat shapes, some hiding coins for luck. When I bit into one, I found nothing inside but laughter and warmth. The family smiled at me, as if I belonged. I thought of our own feasts in the valley—drums beating, men dancing, women singing, food shared until everyone's stomach was full. Different rituals, different songs, but the same spirit of hope for a new year.

Outside, fireworks exploded across the sky. The sparks lit up the snow, turning the world into fire and ice. I stood there, tears freezing on my cheeks, whispering: Even far from home, people carry the same longing for joy, for togetherness, for tomorrow.

After the snow and fire of Jilin, Zhejiang felt like warmth again.

In Hangzhou, I walked by West Lake. The water was calm, the surface glimmering like silk. Willows bent low, their branches brushing the lake as if whispering secrets. Boats drifted slowly, their lanterns swaying.

A woman selling silk scarves saw my bilum bag and laughed kindly. She draped a scarf across my shoulders, soft and shining. "Beautiful," she said. I smiled and told her about my mother, who bent daily over kaukau vines, planting, weeding, harvesting. She told me of her family, weaving silk from threads spun by worms.

Our lives seemed different, yet I felt the closeness of women's labour. Her silk, my harvest—both gifts of hands that never rest.

At dawn, I watched fishing boats return to shore. Their decks glittered with silver fish. Men shouted cheerfully as they lifted baskets, their faces lined with sea-wind. It reminded me of men in my valley returning from hunts with cassowaries or pigs. Wherever we live—by sea, by river, by mountain—we feed our people, we share food, we celebrate survival.

That evening, I sat by the lake, the scarf still on my shoulders, and whispered: Everywhere, life is a rhythm. Work, share, eat, rest, dream. Rivers or valleys, seas or mountains—the heart beats the same.

From Zhejiang's gentle lakes, my journey carried me west to Gansu.

Gansu was a land of contrast—deserts stretching bare, mountains rising sharp, wind sweeping dry across the skin. The earth here felt older, harsher, as though it had seen too many centuries and carried their weight. My valley is green and soft with gardens, but Gansu's face was tough, carved by time and struggle.

Near Dunhuang, I visited the Mogao Caves. At the entrance, the wind carried sand that stung my cheeks, but inside, the air grew cool and still. On the walls, I saw Buddhas painted in rich colours, their faces calm and watchful. Some had survived over a thousand years. The pigments glowed faintly in the dim light, as if they carried whispers from the past.

I thought of our own body painting in Huli. Our colours fade quickly, washed away by rain or sweat. They exist for the moment—for one ceremony, one battle, one dance. Then they vanish, leaving only memory. But here, art endured. The painted Buddhas had outlived their makers, outlived dynasties. I touched the air before them, my hand trembling. Prayer, I realised, takes many forms. Some last a night. Some last a thousand years.

Leaving the desert, I felt the weight of silence in my bones. Yet silence teaches too. It tells us to listen—to earth, to ancestors, to ourselves.

From Gansu, I travelled to Henan, the cradle of much of China's history.

Here I met the Yellow River, the "Mother River." Its waters rolled muddy and strong, carrying life and burden. People told me it fed the earliest Chinese civilisations. Standing on its banks, I thought of mothers in my valley. They feed us, clothe us, carry heavy loads, and often suffer in silence. The Yellow River was the same—giving, sustaining, yet heavy with sacrifice.

In Henan, I visited the Shaolin Temple. Monks in orange robes moved with strength and precision. They leapt, spun, and struck the air in movements both fierce and graceful. I watched, wide-eyed, as their bodies became prayers in motion. Their discipline was not for show; it was devotion, a way of life.

I thought of the men in my valley, training in the forest. Their movements are not smooth like the monks, but born from need—hunting, fighting, surviving. Strength, I saw, takes many forms. Whether in kung fu or in stalking cassowary, both are offerings of the body to something greater.

From Henan, I went north to Hebei.

Hebei's fields stretched wide, smoke curling from the chimneys of villages. The land felt open, less crowded than Beijing or Shanghai. Apples hung in orchards, red and bright. I bit into one, its taste sharp, sweet, and fresh, the juice dripping down my chin. It reminded me of guava picked fresh in the valley, eaten under the shade of a tree. Simple fruits, yet both carried the joy of earth's generosity.

I walked a section of the Great Wall here. Stone stretched across the mountains like a scar, winding endlessly. Each brick, each stone, laid by human hands long gone. I thought of fences in our valley—built with sticks, vines, and stones to protect gardens. The Great Wall was much larger, built to defend a nation. Yet the heart behind it was the same: fear, care, hope for survival. People everywhere build walls, whether of stone or of wood, to protect what they love.

From Hebei, I continued east to Jiangsu.

Jiangsu was alive with rivers and canals. In Nanjing, I walked along the Qinhuai River at night. Red lanterns floated above the water, their reflections shimmering. Music drifted through the streets, mingling with the scent of roasting chestnuts. I walked slowly, letting the warmth of sound and smell carry me.

In my valley, nights are quiet, filled only with drums, insects, and the murmur of fire. Here, nights pulsed with human energy, with laughter, with songs in a language I did not know. Yet I felt the same pull of night—the invitation to reflect, to gather, to remember that we are human together.

I thought of my mother sitting by the fire, telling stories. The lanterns here seemed to hold the same purpose—light in the darkness, warmth for the heart.

From Jiangsu, I travelled north again, to Liaoning, a land shaped by cold seas.

In a fishing village, the air smelled of salt and brine. Fishermen returned from the sea, their faces weathered, their hands quick and sure. They cracked open crabs, pried apart shells, and invited me to taste. I hesitated, then sucked the sweet, salty meat from the claws. The taste was strong, alive with the ocean.

It reminded me of feasts in my valley, where men shared roasted pig, women passed kaukau, and children licked fat from their fingers. The sea or the land—it makes no difference. Food, shared in laughter, binds a community.

I watched a fisherman repair his nets, fingers moving, steady and practiced. I thought of my aunt plaiting bilums, her hands weaving life into every loop. Nets, bilums—both tools of survival, both born from patience and skill.

As the cold wind whipped my face, I whispered: We live in different lands, but our labours are the same. Our hands tell our stories. Our hands keep us alive.

From the cold seas of Liaoning, my path went southward to Guangdong.

Guangdong's air was different—warm, thick, full of life. The markets here overflowed with colours. Stalls carried fruits I had never seen before: spiky durians, star-shaped carambola, dragon fruits glowing pink and green. Their smells mixed with frying oil, roasted meats, and the chatter of thousands of voices.

In a teahouse, I experienced dim sum. Dish after dish arrived—steamed dumplings, buns filled with sweet red bean, slippery rice rolls, chicken feet cooked tender with spices. It was not one big meal but many small tastes, each carrying its own story. People laughed, shared plates, poured tea for each other. I thought of our mumu feasts back home, where meat, kaukau, and greens are cooked in the earth oven, then shared among kin. Different foods, same spirit: to eat together is to be alive together.

Walking through the old villages of Guangdong, I saw houses built with earth and stone, walls curved inward, protecting families across generations. Beside them rose towers of glass, flashing neon lights at night. Old and new stood side by side. I realised then that survival is not only about holding on to the past—it is also about learning to walk with change.

From Guangdong, I took a ferry to Hong Kong.

The city appeared suddenly, rising from the water like a forest of glass and steel. Skyscrapers pierced the sky, jagged and sharp, their windows glowing like stars. The streets pulsed with people, their feet hurrying, their screens glowing in their palms.

At first, I felt lost, as if swallowed by a giant creature. But then, in the small corners, I found the city's heart. I entered Wong Tai Sin Temple, where incense smoke curled into the sky. Worshippers bowed, their hands clasping sticks of burning incense. The air smelled sweet, heavy with devotion. I closed my eyes and prayed too—not to their gods, but to mine. I asked the spirits of my valley to guide me, even here, between towers.

In Central, I walked narrow streets where old markets still lived. Women sold vegetables, fish, and herbs. Above them, neon signs blinked in red and green. I tasted egg tarts, their crusts flaky, their custard golden and sweet. I laughed at the surprise of them—so simple, yet so comforting.

At night, I took a tram up to Victoria Peak. From there, I looked down on the entire city. Lights stretched like stars fallen to earth, rivers of gold winding through darkness. Yet even in its glitter, Hong Kong reminded me of my own mountains. Looking down humbles the heart. Whether gazing from Victoria Peak or from the ridges of Tari, the message is the same: the world is wide, and we are small.

From Hong Kong, I crossed by ferry to Macau.

Macau carried another rhythm entirely. Here, Portuguese tiles patterned the ground, bright and intricate. Old churches stood in ruins, their stone walls whispering centuries of trade, colonisation, and cultural blending. At the Ruins of St. Paul's, I ran my fingers along the stone, feeling history pressed into every crack.

But Macau was not only about the past. Casinos rose high, flashing lights throughout the night. Inside, people laughed, shouted, cried, chasing luck in spinning wheels and falling cards. It was a different kind of ceremony; one I did not know well. Yet even here, I sensed the same hunger humans everywhere carry—the desire for more, the dream that tomorrow may change in an instant.

In Senado Square, music filled the air. Children chased pigeons, their arms flapping like wings. Vendors sold Portuguese egg tarts, warm from the oven. I bit into one, the crust buttery, the custard creamy, and I laughed again—so much like the Hong Kong tarts, yet carrying its own flavour. Here cultures had collided and created beauty, just as our clans in Papua New Guinea sometimes join through marriage, exchange, and friendship.

By the time I left Macau, I felt full—not only from the food but from the stories of all these places. I carried fifteen faces of China in my heart.

On the plane home, I pressed my forehead against the window. Below me, the patchwork of rivers, mountains, and cities grew small, shrinking into mist. I remembered the ferris wheel in Tianjin, the silent Buddhas of Gansu, the frozen laughter of Jilin's New Year, the shimmering lights of Hong Kong.

Travel had shown me not only new lands but new corners of my own heart.

In every province, every city, I had found echoes of my valley. Markets filled with bargaining voices. Mothers' hands shaping food. Children's laughter rising like birds. Men carrying the weight of survival. Women carrying the quiet strength of tomorrow.

Distance dresses the heart in new clothes, but it does not change its beat.

When the silver bird descended toward the mountains of Koroba, mist rose again, wrapping the ridges in its arms — just as it had when I was a child. I stepped out and smelled the damp earth, the smoke of cooking fires, the sweet scent of kaukau gardens. My people greeted me with smiles, curious eyes, and the warmth of belonging.

I told them stories of rivers wider than our valleys, of towers touching the sky, of snow that falls like ash from heaven. They listened, eyes wide, laughing, questioning, dreaming. And as I spoke, I realised the journey was not mine alone anymore. It now belonged to all of us.

Travelling through China had been like walking through a great woven mat, each thread a city, a river, a tradition, a hope. I, a Huli woman from Papua New Guinea, had walked those threads and become part of the pattern.

That night, as stars glittered above the valley, I whispered to the sky, the rivers, the ancestors, and the wind:

Thank you for showing me the world. May I carry it gently, and may it carry me well.

14

YIWU MARKET: EXPLORING THE WORLD'S WHOLESALE GIANT

When I first heard that I would be visiting Yiwu, my heart raced with anticipation. Yiwu is a name that carries weight far beyond China: it is the world's largest wholesale market, where goods flow daily in unimaginable quantities, and traders from every continent meet in one place. I had read about it online, in newspapers, and through stories from students who had visited before, but nothing could prepare me for the reality of stepping inside that massive, humming expanse. It felt as if the entire world had been compressed into a city of stalls and shops, stretching endlessly beyond my sight.

I arrived early, before the market fully opened, walking along streets alive with movement. Trucks rattled past, some stacked with crates so high I wondered how they stayed balanced. People carried boxes on carts, their hands and feet moving in practiced rhythm. The air smelled faintly of paper, plastic, and spices. I clutched my bilum tightly, feeling my home in Hela with me, anchoring me amid the unfamiliar chaos. I whispered softly, "Here we go. The world is waiting."

When the gates opened, I stepped inside, and the scale of Yiwu struck me. The market was organised into districts: textiles, electronics, toys, jewelry, kitchenware, decorations, and more. Each aisle seemed endless. Fluorescent lights made every colour bright and vivid. People spoke dozens of languages, negotiating, laughing, gesturing. Chaos and order danced together, creating a pulse I could feel in my chest.

I wandered first into the textiles section. Rolls of silk, cotton, polyester, embroidered and printed, were stacked floor to ceiling. I ran my fingers across the fabrics, thinking of the bilums and tapa cloths of Popondetta, woven carefully with meaning. Both fabrics carried stories, though one told of home and identity, the other of trade and global connection. I realised that even in this modern, global space, there was a subtle reminder of the power of threads, of weaving, of human intention.

A group of African traders caught my eye. They were negotiating with a Chinese wholesaler over large quantities of shirts. Gestures flew, voices rose, and laughter punctuated the discussion. One man held up a shirt, scrutinised it, and frowned. The seller replied, pointing to stitching and material. I smiled to myself. Even in worlds apart, the rules of negotiation were universal. I thought of pig exchanges in Hela, ceremonies where trust and respect were built through negotiation. The goods differed, the currencies changed, but human relationships remained the same.

In the electronics section, I discovered aisles of mobile phones, chargers, headphones, and robotic toys. I held a small device that could track health and temperature. I marveled at its design. In Hela, our inventions are simpler: traps for hunting, planting tools, and ways of reading the weather. Yet the human impulse is the same—to solve problems, to make life easier, to innovate. I pressed the device into my palm and thought, "Our minds, whether in the highlands or in a market like this, reach for the same sky."

By mid-morning, Yiwu had grown crowded. Families and small-business owners arrived to purchase wholesale goods. Children tugged at their parents' hands, delivery workers dashed through aisles. I wandered to the toy section, admiring the colourful dolls, building blocks, and electronic pets. I smiled, thinking of Hela children who make toys from bamboo and cloth scraps. Creativity is universal; available resources shape it differently.

At a small stall selling trinkets—keychains, ornaments, souvenirs—I was noticed by a young man. "Where are you from?" he asked. "Papua New Guinea," I answered. His eyes widened. "Ah! South Pacific! Island girl!" I laughed. We began gesturing and talking about popular export items to Africa, the Middle East, and Europe. I marveled at the speed at which products moved from imagination to reality and then onto the world stage. I thought again of Hela: slow, deliberate, patient. Here, speed ruled, yet the human principles remained the same: work hard, connect, and deliver.

Lunch brought me to a small food court. The aromas of dumplings, noodles, roasted meats, and fried rice filled the air. I sat near the window, watching the flow of people outside. Trucks moved past, workers carried goods, and buyers negotiated. I felt both small and part of something immense. Yiwu is not just a market—it is a living organism, pulsing with ambition, invention, and connection. I thought of Hela markets, smaller and quieter, but rich with stories and human bonds. Yiwu was larger, but the principle was identical: commerce is about connection, trust, and purpose.

After lunch, I wandered through jewelry aisles, fascinated by earrings, necklaces, and bracelets glittering under the lights. I picked up a carved wooden necklace, red and black, and pressed it to my chest. It reminded me of Huli ornaments worn during *singsings*. Fashion tells a story, whether in Yiwu or Hela. Identity travels through colours, shapes, and materials.

As the day progressed, I moved through kitchenware, stationery, and home goods. I paused frequently, watching people negotiate, exchange money via mobile phone, and transport enormous quantities of items effortlessly.

Yiwu is called the world's market, and I understood why. It is a place where globalisation, creativity, and human ingenuity converge. I thought of PNG, where markets are smaller, slower. Yet even in the highlands, people create, connect, and trade. Yiwu simply magnified the same principles millions of times.

On my second day, I returned to explore the foreign trade section. Here, traders from Africa, the Middle East, Europe, and Southeast Asia interacted with Chinese sellers. I watched a Moroccan man negotiating for fabrics, pointing at a pattern and shaking his head. A Chinese seller explained patiently, gesturing toward colour and texture. I realised that trade is not just about price—it is about understanding, respect, and communication. My mind drifted to Hela, where elders mediate disagreements and negotiate clan boundaries. The principles are identical: listen, speak, and honour trust.

I spent hours watching packaging operations. Goods moved along conveyor belts, scanned, labeled, and packed for shipment worldwide. It was mesmerising. Each item that passed through hands, machines, and boxes would reach a new country, a new home. I thought of Hela gardens: the careful planting of kaukau, the nurturing of crops, and the eventual sharing of food. The scales differ, but the essence is the same—care, preparation, and distribution to sustain life.

Lunch that day was simple, yet unforgettable. I sat on a bench in a quiet corner, eating dumplings, and observed a small child selling candy alongside his mother. His voice, high and persistent, cut through the ambient noise. I smiled, thinking of Hela children selling small bundles of greens or fruits in local markets. The energy, determination, and courage to engage with the world was universal.

By the third day, I allowed myself to follow a few international buyers more closely, observing their strategy, negotiation, and patience. They carried lists, measured goods, and tested quality meticulously. I noted how their attention to detail reminded me of the elders in Hela, who examine a pig before approving it for bride price or a ceremonial exchange. Different items, different currencies, but the same careful observation and respect for value.

I returned to the textiles section again, this time noting patterns intended for African markets. I held a length of cloth against my arm and imagined it draped in Lagos or Nairobi. Each pattern carried an intention, a story, a cultural meaning. I thought of Hela bilums and tapa cloths, each designed for ceremony, each carrying history and identity. Threads connect people, regardless of geography.

The food stalls within Yiwu became my small sanctuary. Each day, I tried new dishes, marveling at the combinations of flavour, spice, and presentation. The dumplings reminded me of roasted kaukau in a mumu: both simple, yet deeply meaningful. They are crafted with care, shared with others, and consumed in community. I thought of the universality of food as a connector, across continents and cultures.

One evening, as I walked back through the streets outside the market, the neon lights reflecting off wet pavement after a brief rain, I paused to reflect on what I had learned. Yiwu is a place of commerce, yes, but also a place of human ambition, adaptation, and imagination. It reminded me that progress is not just about wealth or scale—it is about vision, coordination, and the willingness to take risks.

I thought deeply about PNG. What could we learn from Yiwu? Perhaps not its size, but its vision, organisation, and speed. Perhaps we could embrace modern systems while keeping our culture intact. We could trade not only in goods but in knowledge, in trust, in human connection. Yiwu had shown me that global commerce is not impersonal—it is about human ingenuity, empathy, and understanding.

By the fourth day, I felt I was becoming part of Yiwu's rhythm. I observed the delivery systems, where workers on e-bikes transported goods in precise timing. I saw robots in restaurants carrying bowls of noodles to tables, bowing with mechanical courtesy. I realised that efficiency and human intention can coexist, creating a system where creativity and labour meet.

In quiet moments, I reflected on myself. Each day in Yiwu reshaped my understanding of the world. I felt both small and capable. The market was vast, yet I could navigate it, observe it, and learn from it. I thought of Hela again—the mountains, the rivers, the gardens—and realised that no matter how far I travelled, the lessons of home travelled with me, enriching my understanding of the wider world.

As my visit ended, I stood at the main exit, watching the crowd continue to flow in and out. I clutched my bilum, now heavy with thoughts, papers, and small souvenirs. Yiwu had taught me patience, observation, humility, and ambition. It had shown me that the world is bigger than I imagined, yet entirely navigable if one moves with care, curiosity, and respect.

On the train back to my dormitory, I pressed the bilum to my chest. I whispered softly, "I have seen the world's market. I have learned. I carry Hela in me. And I can carry this knowledge forward." The city lights blurred past the window, merging with the stars above, and I realised that travel is not just about seeing, but about absorbing, reflecting, and becoming.

Yiwu had changed me. It had shown me that commerce is not only about goods—it is about connection, culture, and humanity. It had reminded me that identity and progress can coexist. And it had given me a vision for the future: one where Papua New Guinea can grow, learn, and engage with the world without losing the essence of who we are.

As I finally lay down to rest, I smiled, thinking of the Hela mountains and valleys, the pigs, the bilums, and the songs.

I realised that the threads of home, commerce, and human ingenuity are all woven together, just like the intricate patterns in Yiwu and the bilums I carry. I whispered to myself, "The world is wide, but we can walk through it, carrying home wherever we go."

PART III

ENCOUNTERS WITH CHINA'S GREATNESS

15

LIFE IN XINXIANG: THE HEARTBEAT OF RURAL CHINA

When I first stepped off the train in Xinxiang, Henan Province, the air cut into my cheeks with a sharpness that reminded me of the cold mornings back home in Hela, when mist and dew hang heavy in the valleys before the sun has the strength to burn them away.

But this was a different kind of cold, one that carried the weight of winter in its bones. My breath rose in visible streams, and I wrapped my scarf tighter around my neck, grounding myself in the newness of the place. Coming from Tianjin, with its neon lights, Tientsin Eye that hummed above the streets, and the rhythm of a city that never seemed to pause, Xinxiang felt like a suspension of time, as though the world here moved in slower, heavier breaths. The streets were narrow, the buildings low, and smoke curled from chimneys in threads of gray that twisted lazily against the pale sky. There was silence, not the oppressive kind, but a silence that came from rhythm—people moving in tune with the land rather than the clock.

I carried with me my bilum, woven with care by women from my clan, dyed with the rich hues of earth, ochre, and forest greens. It was a piece of Hela that I never travelled without, a reminder of where my story began. In it I carried not only small belongings but also my intention: a gift for my friend's mother, who had invited me into her home for the winter holidays. I knew that the bilum would speak more eloquently than my Mandarin, still clumsy and hesitant. It carried within its weave the hands of my people, their patience, their rhythm, their stories. I wanted it to bridge the distance between my mountains and this flat, frost-covered land in Henan.

From the first step into the village, I felt the weight of eyes upon me. Children stopped mid-play, their laughter freezing into silence as they turned to stare. Their small hands hung in the air, suspended, as though uncertain whether to wave or retreat. Women carrying baskets paused at doorways, tilting their heads in quiet amazement. Men, bent over hoes or standing by sheds, straightened momentarily, their gaze fixed on me with curiosity that was neither hostile nor welcoming, but searching. I knew what it meant to be the only Black person in a place where the world outside had not yet arrived in full force. Their eyes traced the contours of my skin, my hair, my stance. I felt exposed and yet also deeply aware of the significance of this moment. In their gaze, I was both stranger and teacher, anomaly and possibility.

I smiled softly and inclined my head in greeting. My steps along the dirt paths were deliberate, respectful, echoing the way I walked through gardens back home—aware that each footprint carried meaning. The earth here was different, harder from frost, but it carried the same sense of sacredness. I reminded myself that as a guest, my first offering must always be humility. With every gaze that lingered, I wrapped my bilum closer to my chest, feeling its texture under my fingers as though it gave me courage, as though it whispered: you are never alone.

When I arrived at my friend's home, her mother greeted me with a mixture of warmth and hesitation. Her eyes flickered over my face, taking in what was new, what was unfamiliar. I could feel her uncertainty, the unspoken questions in her silence. Slowly, with both hands, I offered her the bilum. I unfolded it carefully, the woven strands stretching open like a story being told. For a moment she looked at it without touching, as though uncertain whether it was truly for her. Then she reached out, her fingers brushing over the weave, tracing its patterns with quiet reverence. A smile, small at first, grew across her face. Her shoulders relaxed, and her eyes softened. She nodded, her gaze meeting mine with recognition. That moment was a bridge. No words were needed. The bilum had spoken: it had told her I came with respect, that I carried the labour of my people as a gift, that I wished to belong, even temporarily, to the rhythm of her world.

The mornings on the farm began before the sun could fully rise. Frost clung to the fields, shimmering like tiny crystals, and my breath hung heavy in the air. My friend led me through the routines, and I found myself immersed in the cadence of rural labour: feeding chickens, carrying buckets of water from the well, checking the narrow irrigation channels for blockages of ice. Each movement required patience, a slowing down of my usual pace, a deep attention to detail.

My hands grew stiff from the cold, but I welcomed the ache, for it grounded me in the work. I thought of Hela then—of my mother and my aunts, bent over gardens, their hands caked with soil, their laughter rising above the ridges as they worked. Though the soil in Xinxiang was different in texture and colour, the spirit of labour was the same. To work the earth is to listen to it, to honour its rhythm, to recognise that sustenance is born from patience, not haste.

At first, the villagers' eyes followed me wherever I went. When I lifted bales of fodder or bent to scatter grain for chickens, their gazes lingered, measuring my movements, perhaps trying to understand what had brought me here. Their looks carried no malice, only astonishment. A foreigner, and not just any foreigner but one whose skin spoke of worlds they had never seen, was among them, carrying water, chopping vegetables, repairing fences.

Slowly, however, something shifted. Labour speaks a universal language. As I moved with steadiness, as I accepted instruction with humility, their suspicion softened into acknowledgment. By the end of the first week, some of the older women even began to offer small corrections, guiding my hands in tasks with gestures, as though initiating me into their rhythm. Children, once frozen with awe, began to run alongside me, daring to ask questions in quick Mandarin, laughing freely when I stumbled in my answers. Some reached out to touch my hands, not out of disrespect but to confirm the reality of what their eyes saw. Over time, their laughter became companionship, their curiosity softened into play.

Evenings were my favorite time. After the long hours of labour, when the sun dipped behind the rooftops and the sky turned from pale blue to deep indigo, we gathered by small fires. The warmth of the flames contrasted with the sharp cold that lingered in the air. My friend's family spoke in bursts of stories, laughter, and sometimes in long silences filled with comfort rather than absence. I added my own stories when I could, speaking of Hela's misted valleys, of pigs that roamed gardens, of rivers that sang their way through mountains.

I told them of our festivals, our *singsings*, our drums that echo across ridges, summoning people from far and wide. Their eyes lit up with fascination, their laughter meeting mine when I mimicked the dances of my people. It was then I understood that stories, like bilums, are carriers. They weave worlds together, creating bridges where none existed before. Across firelight, across accents and gestures, we wove ourselves into shared humanity.

I remember one particular morning vividly. I was repairing a fence when I paused to look over the rooftops of the village. Smoke rose in steady streams into the cold air, children chased one another along dirt paths, chickens scratched at the frozen ground. Everything moved with a subtle, almost invisible rhythm of connection—people, animals, land, season, all bound together in unspoken understanding. Standing there, aware of my difference, I realised that to belong is not always about sameness.

Sometimes it is about finding resonance, about contributing presence and labour to the rhythm of a place. Though I remained the only Black person in the village, I felt less like an outsider and more like a thread woven, however temporarily, into their fabric.

Each day carried with it a meditation. Feeding the chickens taught me consistency—how small acts repeated daily sustain life. Clearing water channels taught me patience—that neglect in small matters leads to greater loss. Harvesting vegetables taught me care—that each head of cabbage, each radish, each carrot carried within it the labour of months. I realised how urban life, with its emphasis on speed and efficiency, often dulls awareness of these truths. In Xinxiang, efficiency was measured not by time saved but by sustainability, by whether tomorrow could be carried forward without exhaustion of land or people. The lesson was profound: progress measured by machines may dazzle, but progress measured by endurance sustains.

Winter nights were long, stretching like silken threads of silence across the village. Wrapped in blankets near a small stove, I would watch the shadows of flames dance on the wooden walls. The creaks of the house, the cluck of chickens, the occasional bark of a dog—all became part of my meditation. I thought often of identity—what it meant to carry my Huli face, my Huli skin, my Huli spirit into a place where I was seen first as 'different'.

The villagers' eyes reminded me that identity is never only what we say of ourselves; it is also what others see, what they project, what they struggle to reconcile. Yet I also realised that identity is not static. It is relational, unfolding through the dance of presence, perception, and shared experience. In Xinxiang, I learned that identity grows not by hiding difference but by allowing it to meet, transform, and be transformed by others.

One afternoon, while preparing cabbage for market, I watched my friend's mother work. Her hands moved with grace born of repetition, each gesture deliberate, each motion efficient. As she washed and bundled the vegetables, I thought of my own mother in Hela, peeling kaukau, arranging produce, guiding children with the same quiet authority. Labour, I realised, carries stories across generations. The hands of mothers are archives — repositories of survival, resilience, and love. To watch her work was to watch history in motion, silent but enduring. My chest swelled with recognition. Though oceans separated us, the spirit of care expressed through work bound us together.

Children were my greatest teachers. Their curiosity knew no boundaries. They followed me, tested me, laughed at me, and taught me without realising it. In their playfulness, they erased distance. In their laughter, they welcomed me. By the second week, their initial awe had melted into ordinary acceptance. They no longer stared at me as an anomaly; they tugged at my sleeves to join games, offered me makeshift toys, asked me to sing songs from my homeland. I taught them Huli words, and they repeated them clumsily, delighting in their unfamiliar shapes. I joined their laughter, grateful for their willingness to weave me into their childhood memories.

The month passed slowly, yet with a fullness that made each day feel complete. Every evening, I reflected on the contrast between rural and urban China. In Tianjin, the world spun with speed — machines, QR codes, lights, and endless motion. In Xinxiang, the world turned with patience — soil, seasons, frost, and care. Neither was superior; both were necessary. One inspired imagination, the other grounded life. Together, they formed the heartbeat of a nation in transformation. For me, the lesson was personal: I, too, needed both. My Huli roots gave me rhythm and endurance; my education in cities gave me vision and possibility. To weave them together was my task.

On my last evening in the village, we gathered once more around the fire. The family shared songs, their voices rising into the night air, carrying warmth into the cold. They invited me to join, and though my voice stumbled, they laughed and encouraged me.

Firelight flickered on their faces, etching them into my memory. I thought then of Hela, of fire circles where we sing our own ancestral songs, and I felt the closeness of worlds that on maps seem distant but in spirit resonate deeply. As the fire crackled, I felt gratitude swell in my chest. Gratitude for the soil, the smoke, the stares, the laughter, the labour, the acceptance.

When the time came to leave, I walked slowly through the village, noticing details I had overlooked before—patterns of footprints in the snow, children's drawings etched into frost on wooden doors, the rhythm of smoke drifting with the wind. I realised that these small details were the heartbeat of the place, the things that sustained life quietly, without grandeur. I offered my bilum once more, reaffirming the gesture of respect and connection. My friend's mother received it, her smile warm, her eyes reflecting recognition beyond words. In that moment, I understood that gifts are not about objects but about presence, acknowledgment, and the weaving of mutual respect.

The train ride back to Tianjin felt like moving from one world into another. The frost-covered fields of Xinxiang receded, giving way to the neon glow of the city. Yet I carried the village with me—not in objects, but in rhythm, in memory, in reflection. I carried the stares of children, the labour of hands, the smell of smoke, the laughter by the fire.

I carried the reminder that identity can be both rooted and open, that difference can be both challenge and bridge. I carried the quiet wisdom of the land, which whispered patience, humility, and respect.

As the train sped forward, I pressed my hand against my bilum, feeling its woven threads under my fingers. I closed my eyes and whispered silently to the mountains of Hela and the frost-covered fields of Xinxiang: "I carry you both. You are woven together in me." And I understood that my journey was not simply about degrees or cities or technologies. It was about weaving — drawing together the threads of experience, of place, of rhythm and wisdom, to create a tapestry that could serve as a guide for me, for my people, and, perhaps, for my nation.

16

WALKING THE GREAT WALL: A TIMELESS JOURNEY

I grew up where the clouds hang low over the mountains, in Hela, where the land is green with gardens and dark with forest, and where our feet learn the feel of steep ridges before our minds even understand balance. I am Huli, a daughter of warriors and gardeners, raised among the *singsing* drums and the red ochre of face-paint, where every step on the earth carries the weight of ancestors.

When I was a girl, I never imagined the stones of another people's mountain would one day lie beneath my feet. I thought the ridges of Hela were the whole world, and that the walls we built were of woven cane and sharpened stakes to keep pigs from the kaukau patches. A wall, to me, was something alive, growing with vines and mended by hand. Yet I heard whispers, through schoolbooks and travellers who passed through Tari, of a wall so vast that it ran across the back of a country larger than the clouds — China. A wall like the spine of a dragon, they said.

I carried that picture in my mind like a dream: a long, unbroken backbone of stone stretching over the world.

Years later, when I stood before that dragon's back, I felt again like a child, small and breathless before something too large to fit into words.

The Great Wall.

It rose from the earth in slabs of grey stone, climbing steep ridges as if even the mountains could not stop it. The cold of Beijing's autumn bit into my bones, but I carried with me the heat of my homeland. I tied a strip of bright bilas cloth around my waist beneath my jacket, a hidden reminder of Huli identity, and with each step I felt my ancestors walking with me.

I began the climb.

The Wall did not roll gently; it leapt up the mountain in uneven stairs, some so steep I had to lift my knee nearly to my chest. My lungs burned, but I smiled. This was not so different from climbing to the high ridges of Hela, where we chased pigs or hunted cuscus in the early morning. My thighs knew this work. My breath remembered it. Yet there was another weight here — the weight of centuries. Each stone carried the handprint of someone long gone, men who hauled rock, women who waited, emperors who commanded. I placed my palm against the cold stone and felt time flow into me.

Climbing the Great Wall, I was not only a visitor. I was a Huli woman carrying my people's spirit onto another people's mountain.

The stones under my feet shifted from smooth to cracked, worn by millions of footsteps before mine. Tourists moved around me — a river of faces, some pale, some dark, some carrying cameras larger than their hands. They panted, laughed, or stopped to catch their breath. But I walked with steady rhythm, the way we Huli women walk long distances to market: one foot after the other, never hurrying, never stopping.

In my mind I carried the voices of my grandmothers. They taught me that the body is not separate from the land, that our bones belong to the ridges we climb, that each step is also an offering. So as I climbed the Wall, I prayed silently. I prayed to the spirits of the mountains of Hela, asking them to join me on this strange mountain of another people, so I would not be alone.

The air was sharp and dry, unlike the heavy, wet air of my home. My lips cracked, and my skin longed for the mist of the Tari basin. But when I reached a high watchtower and looked out, the sight filled me with wonder. The Wall stretched across the ridges like the backbone of some great beast, rolling away into the horizon, folding itself into valleys and climbing out again. I had never seen anything so stubborn, so determined. Even the mountains seemed unable to break it.

I thought of our Huli walls — short, fragile, meant only to keep pigs away from gardens. They are built quickly, patched often, and always need watching. But this wall-----this wall was built not to keep pigs out, but to keep armies out. It was not woven with bush rope but carved from stone and sweat. And it had lasted through centuries.

A man in a red cap passed me, smiling. "Ni hao," he said, nodding.

I answered with a nod and a smile. I did not know his language, but I knew his smile. The Wall, I realised, was not only stone but a gathering of people. All of us came from far corners of the earth, climbing the same stairs, breathing the same thin air.

Halfway up a particularly steep rise, my legs trembled. The stone steps were uneven, and I had to grip the railing. Sweat trickled down my back beneath my jacket. For a moment, I thought of stopping, of sitting down among the other climbers who rested and drank water from bottles. But then I remembered the Huli way: when a woman carries a bilum heavy with sweet potatoes, she does not stop halfway up the ridge. She sings quietly to herself, she keeps the beat of her feet, and she reaches the top because food must reach the family.

So I sang. Softly, so only I could hear. A Huli tune, one my mother used to hum while we dug kaukau. The melody gave me strength.

Step by step, I climbed.

When I reached the next watchtower, my chest opened with pride. I had not only climbed the Wall; I had carried with me the sound of my homeland. I leaned against the window of the tower, looking out at the hills of China, and imagined for a moment that I was standing on the ridges of Hela, looking down into Tari. The valleys might be different, the houses not of kunai grass but of concrete, yet the rhythm of mountains was the same. Mountains speak to each other, I thought. Perhaps the mountains of Hela and the mountains of China have always whispered across the seas, and now I was the messenger walking between them.

I ran my hand along the stone ledge. Cold. Hard. Eternal.

And yet, as I touched it, I thought of impermanence. Even the greatest stone will one day crumble. Even the longest wall cannot hold back time. My people teach that life is fragile, that even the strongest warrior can fall in battle, that beauty fades and bones return to the earth. The Great Wall, too, carries this truth. It is strong, yes, but I could see cracks between the stones, weeds pushing through, moss creeping along the edges. Time is patient. It will wait until even the dragon's spine is dust.

This thought did not make me sad. It comforted me. For if even the Wall must one day fall, then my smallness, my struggles, my fleeting breath were not shameful. We are all carried by time, great or small.

I began to climb again.

With every step, I felt myself less a visitor and more a witness. The Wall was not only China's. It belonged to all who had seen it, touched it, carried its memory back to their own people. One day, when I returned to Hela, I would tell my children and grandchildren that I climbed the Great Wall. Not as a tourist with a camera, but as a Huli woman carrying the spirit of her mountains onto the stones of another land.

And in that way, the Wall became part of me.

The higher I climbed, the thinner the air felt. My lungs strained, my heart beat loudly in my ears, but I welcomed the rhythm. In Hela, we measure strength not by smoothness of breath, but by how much we can endure without stopping. To feel the burn in my chest was to feel alive.

I pressed on, past groups of tourists who rested on the steps. Some looked at me with curiosity — perhaps because of the bilas cloth peeking from under my jacket, its bright pattern unlike anything they knew. I saw one young girl point and whisper to her mother, who smiled at me warmly. I smiled back. I wished I could tell them who I was, that I came from a place far away, a place where mountains wear crowns of cloud, where people still sing to the land. But I carried that story in silence. My steps were my language.

The stairs became steeper again. My thighs ached, and I leaned forward, pressing my palms against my knees with each push upward. The stones were uneven — some tall, some shallow, some broken. It was not a climb that offered mercy. And yet, in its hardness, it reminded me of home.

In the highlands of Hela, there are ridges so sharp that the ground falls away on both sides. When you climb them, your heart is in your throat, but your feet keep going because you trust the mountain. That same trust carried me here. I trusted the Wall would hold me, just as I trusted the ridges of my homeland. I trusted that my ancestors, though far from their earth, walked with me.

When I reached another tower, I stopped and looked out again. The view spread endlessly — the Wall curling like a grey snake across the horizon, the hills rolling like waves of a green sea. I thought of the stories my elders told around the fire: of the great python spirits that live in rivers, of the warriors who once built trenches across ridges to defend their land. Here in China, the people had done the same, but on a scale so vast it made me dizzy.

I rested my hand on the stone, rough beneath my palm. "Emperor," I whispered, though I did not know which one had ordered this section. "Your people built this. My people also build. We build gardens, we build fences, we build songs. Our walls are not so large, but they are strong enough to keep our pigs from eating our food."

I laughed softly at my own words; the sound lost in the wind. The Wall may have been built for emperors, but I climbed it as a gardener's daughter. The pride of my people came not from ruling over millions, but from planting sweet potatoes deep in the soil, from tending pigs until they grew fat, from walking ridges with strong legs and steady hearts.

And yet, standing here, I felt no smallness. The Wall was vast, but so was my spirit.

I thought of the *singsing* festivals back home, where Huli men paint their faces in bright yellow and red, don wigs of human hair, and dance until the ground shakes. They dance to show strength, to call the spirits, to remind the land that the people are alive. In that moment, on the Wall, I felt as if I, too, was part of a great *singsing*. The Wall itself was the kundu drum, stretching across mountains, beating out the rhythm of centuries. And I, a lone Huli woman, was one of many dancers moving across its length, each of us leaving our mark in footsteps instead of song.

I began to climb again, but slower now, savouring each step. I no longer felt hurried to "reach the top." The climb itself was the meaning. Each stone was a lesson. Each breath was a reminder of life.

At one steep rise, my legs trembled so much that I stopped and leaned against the wall. The cold stone pressed against my cheek. Closing my eyes, I remembered carrying firewood as a girl. My bilum strap cut into my forehead, and my back ached, but my mother walked ahead without complaint, so I followed her. "Strength is not loud," she told me once. "Strength is quiet. Strength is walking when your body says stop."

So I walked again. Quietly. Strongly.

Near the top, the crowd thinned. Fewer people had the stamina to climb that far, and suddenly the Wall felt wide and empty around me. The silence was heavy, broken only by the whistle of wind and the beat of my heart. I placed my hands on the stone railing and looked out over the mountains.

It was then that tears came, unbidden. Not of sadness, but of fullness. I thought of my mother in her garden, my father walking to market, my grandparents who never left the highlands of Papua New Guinea. None of them had seen this wall. Yet through me, they were here. My footsteps carried them. My eyes were their eyes. My breath was their breath.

I whispered in Huli: *"Ina okoria kema, ina okoria kema, ina okoria kema"* — *We are here, we are here, we are here.*

The Great Wall stood silent, but I felt it listening.

The Wall pulled me higher, as if testing me, as if asking: How much of yourself can you bring to me?

My legs were heavy, my chest wide with breath, but my spirit felt lighter the further I climbed. The air was colder now, sharp against my skin, but that cold only made me remember the warmth of the highland sun back home. It was strange — how far from Hela I was, and yet how near it seemed, tucked inside my body, stitched into every breath.

A group of men passed me on the steps, talking in quick, musical bursts of Mandarin. They climbed quickly, laughing, as if racing each other. I smiled at their energy. When I was younger, my brothers did the same on our ridges. They would dare each other to run to the top of the hill without stopping, their laughter echoing through the valley. I was smaller, slower, but stubborn. I would climb at my own pace, and though I came last, I always reached the top. That stubbornness was with me now.

The steps tilted steeply upward, narrow, each one a sharp rise. I leaned forward, almost on all fours, climbing like an animal. My breath came in sharp pulls. My jacket grew damp with sweat, though the air was cold enough to numb my fingertips. I thought of the men who had built this wall — how many hands must have bled here; how many bodies had fallen. I wondered if they sang while they worked, as we Huli sing when we garden, or if their voices were swallowed by silence and command.

At a landing, I paused to rest. I pressed my palm against the stone wall beside me. It was rough and uneven, not polished. Each groove told of labour, of chisel, of centuries of wind and rain. My fingers traced the cracks, and I thought of the scars on my father's arms, cut from years of carrying bush knives and firewood. Stone holds memory, just as skin does.

Below me, the view stretched wide — the Wall unraveling down the mountain, dotted with tiny figures moving like ants. Above me, the steps kept climbing, winding toward another tower. I felt caught between two eternities: the long stretch of history behind me, and the endless climb ahead.

I lifted my head and continued upward.

Every few steps, my body cried out: stop, rest, sit down. But my spirit whispered louder: walk, walk, walk. That voice was the same one I had heard as a child carrying kaukau in a bilum, the strap biting into my forehead. It was the voice of my mother, the voice of my grandmothers, the voice of every Huli woman who carried weight up a mountain without complaint.

"Strength is walking when your body says stop."

I repeated her words under my breath, a chant, a rhythm, until my steps found a new beat.

At another tower, I leaned against the window slit and looked out. The land beyond was rolling, endless, mountains folding into valleys. The Wall flowed across them, not straight, but bending, curving, like a living thing. In that moment, it looked less like a wall and more like a river frozen in stone.

I closed my eyes and imagined the Wall as a river, and myself a canoe paddling upon it. The current pulled me forward, carrying me into the unknown. I thought of the Hewa people in the forests beyond Hela, who travel by canoe on the rivers of the lowlands. My people, too, though highland dwellers, know what it means to follow a path that nature itself has carved. This wall was another path — not of water, but of stone.

As I climbed again, I began to count my steps. Not in English. Not in numbers. But in memories.

One step: the smell of smoke from my grandmother's firepit. Another step: the laughter of my cousins running barefoot. Another: the feel of mud between my toes after rain. Another: the song of the kundu drum, deep and steady.

With each step, I carried Hela upward. By the time I reached the next steep flight, I was no longer alone. My valley, my people, my ancestors were all climbing with me, woven into my breath.

Near the top, the crowd was sparse. Only a few walkers moved slowly, pausing often. The silence between us felt sacred. The wind howled across the stones, lifting my hair, tugging at my jacket. I stopped and spread my arms wide, letting the cold air wash over me.

It felt like a *singsing* without drums — the wind itself was the drumbeat, the Wall the dancing ground, and my heartbeat the song.

Tears pricked my eyes again. I was not crying for struggle or pain, but for the largeness of it all. To stand here, a Huli woman from Hela, on the spine of China's dragon, was to stand in the middle of history, in the middle of the world. My people, often unseen by the world, were present here through me. I felt both small and vast at once.

I whispered to the Wall:

"You have seen emperors, soldiers, invaders. Today, you see me. Remember me too."

Then, with slow, reverent steps, I climbed the final rise toward the highest tower.

The final steps were narrow and cruelly steep, each one taller than my knee. My body protested. My thighs quivered, my calves burned, my breath became ragged. But the stones did not yield, and neither did I. I gripped the railing and pulled myself upward, one trembling step at a time.

It was not so different from climbing the highest ridges in Hela, when the grass cuts your legs and the mud sucks at your ankles, when each step feels like your last — and then you find another. I remembered those climbs with my bilum strap pressed against my forehead, the weight of kaukau digging into my shoulders. Every Huli woman knows that pain. Every Huli woman also knows the pride that follows, standing on a ridge with food for the family, looking down at the valley she has conquered.

So I carried that memory into these steps. Each stone became a kaukau. Each breath became a bilum strap. Each moment of weakness became another chance to say: *Ina okoria kema* — we are here.

And then — the final rise opened into a flat space. The highest tower.

I stepped through its arched doorway, and the wind struck me full in the chest. Strong, sharp, whistling around the stone edges. I staggered, then steadied myself, spreading my arms wide as if to embrace the horizon.

The world stretched out before me.

The Wall wound away in both directions, up and down the ridges, over valleys, across horizons so distant my eyes could barely follow. Mountains rolled like sleeping giants beneath a blanket of green and brown. The sky was pale blue, scattered with clouds like brushstrokes.

For a moment, I forgot to breathe.

All the weight of climbing, all the ache in my legs, all the burn in my lungs — it disappeared in that view. What remained was silence and vastness.

I pressed my hand against the cold stone of the tower. I closed my eyes. And I wept.

Not from exhaustion. From recognition.

This wall, though foreign, spoke the same language as the ridges of Hela. It carried the same message: You are small, but you belong. You are brief, but you are part of something eternal.

I thought of my mother bending over her garden, her hands in the soil. I thought of my father carrying firewood along the ridge. I thought of my grandparents who never left the highlands but whose strength carved paths for me. None of them had seen this wall. None had stood here. But I was their daughter, their blood, their memory. Through me, they looked upon it. Through me, they touched it.

I whispered their names one by one into the wind, letting the sound carry across the mountains of China.

The wind answered with its howl, as if carrying their names back to me.

I stood there a long time, feeling the weight of centuries beneath my feet and the breath of my ancestors within my chest. I thought of the emperors who had commanded the Wall, the soldiers who had defended it, the invaders who had tested it. Their stories were written in these stones. But so was mine now. A Huli woman from Hela, far from her own ridges, had climbed here too.

I took a strip of bilas cloth from my pocket — bright, woven, the kind we wear at *singsing*. I tied it gently to the railing at the edge of the tower. The cloth fluttered in the wind, red and yellow against grey stone. Not as a mark of conquest, but as a whisper: We were here too. Hela has touched you. Remember us.

For a long while, I stood there watching it dance, feeling my chest swell with both pride and humility. The Wall did not need me. It would stand long after I was gone. But for one brief moment, it carried me, and I carried it.

Then, slowly, I began the descent. My legs trembled, but my heart was strong.

The wind at the summit was not just wind. It carried voices.

I felt them as much as I heard them: the whispers of those who built this wall, the cries of soldiers who once guarded it, the laughter of children who played in its shadow. And mingled with them, I heard the murmur of my own people — the *singsing* drums, the chants of warriors, the quiet hum of my mother digging kaukau.

Two worlds, distant and different, met in my chest.

I closed my eyes and let the sound wash over me. I thought: This is why I came. Not only to see the stones with my eyes, but to feel them with the whole of myself.

When I first heard of the Seven Wonders, they seemed like names from another universe: pyramids, statues, temples, walls. Places too far, too mighty, too foreign. I, a girl from Hela, walking barefoot on muddy ridges, never imagined I would stand at any of them. And yet here I was — not dreaming, but breathing on the back of the dragon.

The Wall humbled me. It told me: You are small. But at the same time, it lifted me. It said: Your smallness is sacred, because you carry a world inside you.

I thought of how the world might see me — just one woman, brown-skinned, from a country many could not even find on a map. But the Wall did not see me as small. The Wall welcomed me as it had welcomed millions before. It asked nothing but footsteps. It gave everything in return: memory, perspective, connection.

I turned in a slow circle, letting my eyes drink the horizon. The Wall ran both ways, dissolving into mist, into distance, into time itself. I knew I could never walk it all. No one could. But I did not need to. To stand here, to climb one section, was enough. The Wall itself taught me that wholeness is not found in grasping everything, but in touching even a fragment deeply.

I reached out and pressed my palm flat against the stone once more. It was cold, solid, eternal. My hand was warm, fleeting, alive. The meeting of the two felt like a conversation across centuries.

"I am here," I whispered in Huli.

And the stone, in its silence, replied: So am I.

The strip of bilas cloth I had tied to the railing flapped wildly in the wind. Watching it dance, I felt a surge of joy. That bright thread was a bridge — from Hela to China, from my ancestors to theirs, from my small life to the endless river of human effort.

I thought of the Seven Wonders not as separate monuments, but as a chain. Each one a bead, threaded together by human hands. Each one different, but each born of the same yearning: to create something larger than ourselves, something that outlives our breath. The Great Wall was China's bead, but now my own spirit had touched it, polishing it with sweat and tears.

The climb had not been easy. But that was the point. Wonders are not meant to be easy. They demand something of us — our breath, our strength, our humility. And in return, they give us back more than we offered.

At the summit, with the world stretched out before me, I felt both emptied and filled. My body was tired, but my heart overflowed.

For a long time, I stood in silence, letting the wind whip my hair, letting the cloth dance, letting my tears dry on my cheeks.

And then, slowly, I turned toward the steps that would take me down.

17

SHANGHAI: SKYSCRAPTERS AND URBAN MARVELS

When the plane descended through the clouds and the first shimmering outline of Shanghai appeared beneath me, I pressed my forehead against the small airplane window and held my breath. The city seemed endless, as though the very earth had given birth to a forest of glass and steel.

Towers glistened under the late afternoon sun, each one thrusting higher than the last, like mountains made by human hands. I felt an ache in my chest, the kind that comes when you stand between awe and fear. For a moment, I thought of my home in Hela, of Tari's valley wrapped by the surrounding mountains, the mist that lay over the ridges in the early morning, and the way the kundu drums echoed during *singsings*.

The contrast was almost unbearable. Back home, the highest structures were the hills and the men's houses with their grass roofs. Here, the horizon itself seemed cut by sharp edges of towers, daring the sky to resist them. I whispered to myself, "I feel like I am entering the future."

The plane touched down, jolting me from my thoughts. My hands instinctively went to the bilum hanging across my chest, the bilum my mother had made and placed into my hands the night before I left for China. She had said softly, "So you will carry a piece of us." The bilum smelled faintly of coconut oil, its woven threads soft but strong. As I stepped into the airport, surrounded by voices speaking Mandarin, English, and many other languages, that bilum anchored me. It reminded me of who I was, even as the ground beneath me shifted into a world I could barely recognise.

The taxi ride from the airport into the city was like travelling through a dreamscape I did not know how to interpret. The car moved swiftly along highways lit with glowing signs, their characters dancing like calligraphy strokes against the night sky. My driver did not speak English, but when I said "Pudong?" he nodded, eyes flicking to me in the mirror with a quick smile. I sat back, pressing my face to the glass, unable to take my eyes away from the endless parade of towers, bridges, and rivers. Back in Hela, the night is thick and quiet, broken only by the occasional barking of dogs or the rhythm of insects. Here, night was not darkness—it was brightness, pulsing, alive.

The neon signs poured colour into the streets, blues and reds so sharp they pierced my eyes. I thought of the firelight flickering on our faces back home when we sat in the women's house telling stories, shadows stretching across the mud walls. Firelight here is gentle, a companion. Light here felt electric, commanding, and insistent, demanding I keep my eyes open.

I could not stay inside my room that first night. My feet itched to walk, to taste this new land. When I stepped onto the streets of Shanghai, I was nearly swallowed by the crowd. People moved with a kind of purpose, each step quick, decisive, as though every minute was calculated. I felt small, almost clumsy, but I forced myself to keep walking, weaving through the crowd with the same determination I had once used to navigate the muddy tracks between villages during rainy season. At one corner, the scent of food pulled me to a small stall. Steam curled into the night air, carrying with it aromas both savoury and strange. The young man behind the stall looked up and asked, "Ni chi ma?" I blinked, not understanding at first, until he lifted a dumpling with his chopsticks and mimed eating. I nodded quickly. "Yes, yes."

He laughed, scooped several dumplings into a paper box, and handed them to me. I bit into the first one too quickly, and hot broth spilled across my tongue. It burned but filled me with warmth. "Good," I said, nodding. He repeated, "Good!" We laughed together, no common language between us but a shared delight. As I stood there chewing, I thought of kaukau roasted in the mumu, the way we dig hot stones from the fire, lay banana leaves, place the pork, kaukau, and greens together, and cover them with earth. That food carries the flavour of smoke, of soil, of togetherness. This dumpling, with its delicate folds and careful preparation, carried the weight of patience and attention to detail. Different worlds, different tastes, yet both rooted in the same truth: food is never just about filling the stomach; it is about connection.

Drawn forward by curiosity, I followed the stream of people until I reached the Bund. There, I stopped in my tracks. The Huangpu River stretched wide before me, its surface shimmering under the light of a thousand lamps. On my side stood historic stone buildings, their carved facades whispering of another century. Across the river, Pudong blazed like a vision of tomorrow: the Shanghai Tower twisted elegantly upward, the World Financial Center cut sharp against the sky, and the Jin Mao Tower shimmered like a pagoda reborn in steel. I gripped the railing, leaning forward as the cool wind brushed my face. My heart pounded as though trying to keep pace with the energy around me. A woman beside me turned, her scarf fluttering, and in hesitant English asked, "Beautiful, yes?"

"Yes," I breathed. "Very beautiful."

For a long moment, we stood side by side, strangers linked only by the shared wonder of the sight before us. I thought of standing on the ridge in Hela, looking out over the valley at dawn, the mountains rising in layers of mist. That view made me feel part of the earth. This view made me feel like I had stepped into another era, as though time itself had bent forward to show me what waited at the edge of humanity's dreams.

The next day, I decided I could not just look at the towers from below—I had to climb into one, to feel its height. I bought a ticket to the Shanghai Tower and stepped into the elevator. It moved so quickly my ears popped, and when the doors opened at the observation deck, the city unfolded beneath me like a living map. Roads traced their paths like veins, lights blinked like stars, and the river curved like a silver serpent. I pressed my bilum against my chest, whispering, "So high." Back home, only the mountains touched the clouds, their peaks sacred, holding the spirits of our ancestors. Here, humans had built their own mountains, rising above the clouds by will and calculation.

A group of students nearby noticed me. One of them asked, "Where you from?"

"Papua New Guinea," I said, smiling.

Their eyes widened. "Ah! South Pacific! Very far!"

"Yes," I laughed. "Very far."

They asked for a photo, and I agreed, standing with my bilum across my shoulder, smiling into their camera. In that moment, I felt like a bridge, my Huli roots stretching back to the highlands and my feet planted in a tower that pierced the Shanghai sky.

Each day I walked endlessly, my feet carrying me deeper into the city. On Nanjing Road, the lights never dimmed, the shops stretched endlessly, and QR codes replaced coins. I watched as parents guided their children into stores where AI-powered toys responded to their voices, lights flashing, screens glowing. In cafés, students whispered into laptops, laughing as images appeared, as though conjured by magic. Everywhere, technology pulsed like blood through the veins of the city. I realised that just as these skyscrapers rose from the soil into the sky, China's technology was rising, climbing into futures we had only begun to imagine.

I thought of Hela, where children still walk miles barefoot to school, their notebooks sometimes shared between three siblings. I thought of the times we waited weeks for government supplies that never came, of the broken computers left in corners of classrooms, gathering dust because no one knew how to fix them. Here, children played with tools of tomorrow. Back home, children still carved toys from bamboo. The contrast did not make me ashamed—it made me determined. It showed me what was possible.

The city taught me in subtle ways. I noticed how quickly people adjusted their rhythm. The subway moved with exact timing, doors opening and closing like clockwork. Crowds flowed in and out, not with chaos but with practiced precision. In Hela, our rhythm was set by the land—when the sun rose, when the pigs were fed, when the rains came. In Shanghai, the rhythm was mechanical, measured in seconds and circuits. I realised both had their wisdom. One taught patience, the other taught efficiency.

I felt the sharp loneliness too. In the middle of a street filled with thousands of people, I felt invisible. No one greeted me with the cheerful "Yu orait?" of Port Moresby or the warm smile of Hela. Here, people rushed past, eyes fixed ahead. At night, when I lay in my room, I longed for the sound of my relatives laughing around the fire, for the kundu drum beating during a *singsing*. Yet loneliness also sharpened me. It forced me to listen more carefully, to observe, to find meaning in the smallest connections—a smile from a vendor, a nod from a passerby, a dumpling shared in laughter.

The longer I stayed, the more the city became a mirror. Shanghai showed me the future, but it also reflected my past. When I looked at the skyscrapers, I thought of the Huli headdresses, towering high with feathers of birds of paradise. Both were attempts to rise higher, to touch something beyond ourselves. When I watched the endless traffic move in neat lines, I thought of our pig exchanges, where each movement, each gift, followed rules handed down by elders. Different forms, same principle: order holds a community together. When I stood in front of glowing advertisements, faces smiling and speaking words I could not understand, I thought of our *singsings*, where dancers painted their faces in bright yellow, red, and white, each colour a message to those who watched. Communication takes many forms—light, colour, sound—but it always seeks to remind us of who we are.

On my last evening, I returned to the Bund. The air was cool, the river alive with reflections. I stood there, bilum slung over my shoulder, and looked again at the old stone buildings on one side and the glittering towers on the other. I saw tradition and modernity standing face to face, not as enemies but as companions. It reminded me of myself: a woman from Hela standing in Shanghai, carrying the strength of her ancestors and the dreams of tomorrow. I realised then that progress is not about choosing between the old and the new. It is about weaving them together, like the threads of a bilum, strong only when each strand is pulled tight beside the others.

I turned to leave, my steps slow but steady. The skyscrapers no longer felt like strangers looming above me. They felt like markers, reminding me of what humanity could achieve when it dared to build, to imagine, to rise. I walked with the knowledge that I carried my mountains inside me. Shanghai had not diminished me—it had awakened me.

And as I disappeared into the river of people, my bilum swaying gently at my side, I whispered once more, "I felt like I was entering into the future."

18

SKYWARD BOUND: MY FIRST RIDE ON A SKYTRAIN

When I think back to the first time I stepped onto a skytrain in China, I remember how my heart beat faster than the wheels of the machine that carried me. I had ridden buses before, and cars, and even planes, but the skytrain was different. It was not simply a way to travel. It was a vision of tomorrow rolling on steel tracks high above the ground. I can still feel the trembling in my chest, the way my hands gripped the edge of my seat as if I were not only moving through space, but through time itself. That day, as the skytrain lifted me into motion, I whispered to myself: I am entering the future.

I had seen videos before, small clips on my phone, of trains gliding above cities. But to watch something on a screen and to live it with your whole body are two very different things. Screens flatten the world; reality wraps around you.

That morning, I had left my dormitory in Wuhan with my bilum slung over my shoulder, its rough string fibers grounding me in the familiar. I remember thinking, "This bilum has carried kaukau in Hela. Today, it carries my notebook and phone in China." It was my way of saying: I am still me, even as I step into something new.

The station itself already felt like another world. Tall glass doors, machines that beeped when people passed their cards, polished floors that shone like rivers of light. I paused before the map of the routes, so many coloured lines weaving like threads on a bilum. For a moment, I felt lost, as if I were a child again, staring at something too big to understand. The names of the stops were written in Chinese characters I was still learning to read, but the lines themselves told a story: a city connected, a people woven together by motion.

When the train arrived, it slid into the station silently, like a breath held and then released. Its body was sleek, silver and blue, shining under the fluorescent lights. The doors opened without anyone touching them. For a second, I hesitated. My feet wanted to step forward, but my mind held back. I thought of my village in Hela, where the only tracks we know are the paths carved by feet and pigs through the grass. There, when you step onto a path, you know exactly where it leads — to a garden, a river, a neighbour's house. But here, I was about to step onto a moving path that carried thousands of strangers every day, a path high above the ground, controlled by systems I could not see.

Still, I moved. My feet carried me in, and the doors closed behind me with a soft sigh. I was inside.

The interior smelled faintly of metal and something clean, almost like rain after it has washed dust from the air. The seats were smooth, lined in rows, filled with people who did not seem amazed at all. They looked at their phones, read books, or simply sat in silence. For them, this was ordinary. For me, it was a revelation. I sat down by the window and pressed my hand against the glass as if to assure myself it was real.

And then it began to move.

The train started gently, almost imperceptibly, but soon I could feel it gaining speed. The world outside shifted, slowly at first, then faster, until the buildings seemed to glide past like shadows. I pressed my forehead to the glass, eyes wide, heart racing. The city unfolded below me, its roads and cars and bicycles flowing like blood through veins. I was above it all, moving not like a pedestrian or even a passenger in a car, but like a bird flying low, guided by invisible wings of steel.

In that moment, a thought rose within me, uninvited but insistent: If my mother could see me now, what would she think?

I imagined her standing in our garden in Hela, mud on her feet, her hands blackened from the earth. She would tilt her head, squinting at the skytrain, perhaps thinking it was some kind of spirit. She would ask, "Is it safe? Does it fall?" And I would answer, "No, Mama. It is strong. It is the way people move in this land." Then I thought of my father, how he once carried me on his shoulders across a swollen river when I was too small to walk. Would he believe that one day his daughter would ride above rivers and streets in a machine that seemed to defy the weight of the earth?

The train curved gently, and the horizon shifted. Tall towers appeared in the distance, their glass bodies catching the sunlight, flashing like knives of light.

Bridges stretched across the river like threads of silver. Below, I could see cars stuck in traffic, moving inch by inch, while I flew above them without effort. A strange feeling rose in me — not arrogance, but wonder. I thought: So this is how time can be saved. This is how a society can leap forward.

I remembered the long walks of my childhood. Hours spent moving from the village to the health post, or from the garden back home. Journeys measured not in kilometers but in tired legs and swollen feet. Here, minutes replaced hours. A trip that might take half a day in Hela was done in the time it takes kaukau to bake in the mumu. My eyes filled with tears, not only of joy but also of sorrow. Why should my people still walk such long distances when the world has found ways to fly on the ground?

As the train glided smoothly, my mind became restless with questions. What would it take for PNG to build something like this? Could we ever? Would the land allow it? Would our politics? Would our people trust it? These questions circled in me like birds, each one sharp with both hope and doubt.

A child sat across from me, swinging his legs, holding a toy train in his hand. He looked at the window, then at his toy, then back at the window. His lips moved as if whispering secrets to himself. I smiled. For him, this ride was already part of his story, something he would never remember as strange. For me, it was a rupture in time, a crossing of worlds. I felt old and young at once, like a grandmother seeing a miracle and like a child discovering magic.

The stations passed quickly, each one announced by a calm, mechanical voice. At first, I struggled to follow, but then I began to recognise patterns. Each stop was another breath in the lungs of the city, another reminder of how life circulates when connections are strong. People got on and off, their movements fluid, practiced. I thought of the clumsy way PMVs load and unload passengers back home, the shouting, the pushing, the waiting. Here, there was order. And in that order, there was speed.

Philosophy crept into me as the train raced forward. I thought: Is progress measured by how fast we move? Or is it measured by how far we can bring our people with us? For what use is speed if only a few enjoy it while the rest remain behind? The skytrain carried everyone: students, workers, elders, children. It was not a privilege of the rich. It was a public promise, fulfilled in steel and glass. That, I realised, was the lesson. Not the machine itself, but the vision that made it belong to all.

I closed my eyes for a moment and let the hum of the train sink into me. The vibration was steady, like a heartbeat not my own. In that hum, I felt the pulse of a nation determined to rise.

The first ride did not end when my feet touched the platform. It lingered in me, vibrating like the echo of a kundu drum long after the last strike. For days, I felt as if my body still carried the rhythm of the train, as if I were still gliding above the city.

That night, when I closed my eyes to sleep, I dreamt that I was floating above Hela, passing over mountains and rivers, watching the villages below. In my dream, the skytrain reached all the way to Tari. My people were climbing aboard with their bilums, their laughter filling the cars, their kaukau and bananas piled in the seats beside them. My heart swelled in that dream, and when I woke, I almost cried, because it was only a dream — but also, perhaps, a seed.

I rode again, and again, each time discovering something new. In the morning, the carriages were full of commuters, men in neat suits, women in smart dresses, students with backpacks heavy on their shoulders. Everyone seemed to move with purpose, their faces set, their eyes fixed on something ahead. I thought: this is what discipline looks like when it is lived, not just spoken. The train was not only a machine of steel; it was also a classroom, teaching patience, teaching order, teaching the art of moving together without chaos. No one pushed, no one shouted. Each passenger seemed to know that their journey was bound to the journeys of others.

One rainy day, I boarded when the city streets were slick with water. From above, I watched the traffic crawl, cars trapped in pools of rain, bicycles splashing through puddles. But in the skytrain, I felt no delay, no wetness, no struggle. We glided above the storm, untouched, as if the rain belonged to another world. And I thought: is this what progress means — to rise above the weight of weather, above the mud, above the forces that once dictated human life? Yet even as I admired it, I reminded myself that rain is not an enemy. In Hela, rain is blessing and burden alike. It nourishes the gardens, fills the rivers, cools the air. To rise above it is to escape one truth, but perhaps also to risk forgetting its gift.

At night, the skytrain became a different experience altogether. The city below glowed with neon, rivers of light running through its veins. Billboards blinked, bridges shone, reflections shimmered on the water. From my seat, it felt as if I were floating through a galaxy of human-made stars. I pressed my hand to the glass again, marveling at how the line between earth and sky seemed to blur. Was I on the ground, or was I already halfway to the heavens? My heart whispered: this is why they call it skytrain — not only because it rides above the streets, but because it awakens the feeling of touching the sky.

And yet, even in that beauty, there was a shadow of longing. I thought of nights in Hela, where the only lights are the fire in our houses and the quiet glow of the moon. No neon, no endless strings of cars. Just silence broken by the call of insects and the rustle of leaves. Which is better — the silence of the village or the pulse of the city? My soul could not decide. Perhaps both are needed, perhaps the future is not about choosing one over the other, but carrying the wisdom of both within us.

Sometimes, as I sat watching the city pass beneath me, I would imagine conversations with my ancestors. I would picture my grandmother sitting beside me, her hair decorated with bird feathers, her face painted in the red and yellow clay of our tribe. She would look out the window and shake her head.

"What spirit carries us so fast?" she would ask. And I would answer softly, "It is not a spirit, Grandmother. It is knowledge, it is discipline, it is the work of many hands." She would fall silent, perhaps still unconvinced, perhaps thinking of the spirits she knew in the mountains. But then, maybe she would smile, proud that her granddaughter could see such things.

On another ride, I imagined my future children sitting beside me, wide-eyed, their small hands pointing at the towers below. What kind of questions would they ask? Would they wonder why their mother once walked barefoot through muddy paths while here children flew above the city? Would they ask why PNG could not yet offer the same? I felt the weight of those imagined questions pressing on me. It was as if the train itself whispered: you have seen the future — now what will you do with it?

The more I rode, the more I realised that the skytrain was not only about transport. It was a meditation on time. In Hela, time stretches. A journey takes as long as your feet can endure. Waiting is part of life; patience is survival.

But here, time was compressed, folded, almost conquered. The skytrain taught me that minutes can hold what once took hours. And that truth unsettled me. Was faster always better? Did speed mean wisdom, or only urgency? Perhaps the lesson was not to worship speed, but to recognise its power and choose carefully when to use it.

There was one evening when I stayed on the train longer than I needed, just to keep moving, just to keep reflecting. I watched faces come and go, strangers living lives I could only guess at. Some looked tired, some joyful, some lost in their phones. And I thought: every passenger carries a world. The skytrain gathers these worlds and moves them together, like a necklace of strung beads.

In that thought, I saw a metaphor for nations. A country is not one story, but millions carried side by side, all needing to move forward together. PNG, too, must learn this: to link our tribes, our provinces, our dreams, as if on a single train, moving with one hum.

Once, the train passed a school playground. I glimpsed children running, their laughter echoing faintly even through the glass. For them, the skytrain overhead was not a wonder, but an ordinary part of the sky. They would grow up with it, as natural to them as rivers are to me. And that struck me deeply.

Wonder fades into normality with each generation. What astonishes me may be mundane to my children. That is why progress must always be renewed, so that each generation has something new to marvel at, something that expands the horizon of possibility.

And then there was the silence. Not silence of absence, but silence of calm. Even as it sped, the skytrain carried a quietness inside. People spoke in low voices, if at all. The hum of the machine was steady, not intrusive. I found myself breathing more slowly, as if the train itself had lent me its rhythm. It was a reminder that speed does not have to be chaotic; it can also be graceful. That, too, is a lesson for PNG. To move fast without disorder, to rise without tearing ourselves apart — this is the kind of progress we must seek.

The more I rode, the more my reflections deepened into philosophy. I began to see the skytrain as a teacher, not just a vehicle. It taught me about connection, about rhythm, about vision. It showed me that the future is not an abstract dream but a concrete possibility, built with steel, discipline, and shared will. It reminded me that my journey as a student in China was not just about degrees but about encounters that reshape the way I see the world.

Each time I stepped off, I felt changed, as if a small piece of tomorrow had lodged itself inside me. And each time, I carried it back to my dormitory, back into my notebook, where

I wrote furiously, trying to capture the lessons before they slipped away. I wrote about roads in PNG that might one day carry trains, about villages linked not only by footpaths but by bridges of knowledge and steel. I wrote about discipline, about unity, about the hum of progress.

But always, I ended my writing the same way: with the image of my people, barefoot and strong, waiting. Waiting for a future that has not yet arrived. Waiting for leaders to dream beyond elections. Waiting for daughters like me to return, carrying not just stories, but visions.

The skytrain became a mirror. In its windows, I saw both what was and what could be. I saw a reflection of myself — a Huli woman stretched between two worlds, carrying both kaukau and QR codes in her story, both mud and neon in her memory. I realised that to ride tomorrow is not only to sit in a machine that glides above the city, but also to accept the responsibility of carrying that vision home.

Even now, years later, when I close my eyes, I can feel that ride. The hum beneath me, the city unfolding, the sky pressing close. I whisper again the words I spoke that first day: I am entering the future. And I know, with certainty, that once you enter the future, you can never go back unchanged.

19

IN THE LAND OF INVENTIONS

During my time in China, I began to see the country not only through its people and landscapes but also through its long and fascinating history of invention. Before coming here, I honestly thought that most great discoveries in the world had come from Europe. That was the way books in Papua New Guinea told the story.

Europeans invented this, Europeans discovered that. Asians, and especially the Chinese, were hardly mentioned at all. It was only when I began living and studying in China that I realised how wrong that view was.

In my classes and in conversations with teachers and friends, I learned that many things we use every day—paper, printing, the compass, gunpowder, paper money, even clocks—were created in China centuries ago.

At first, it was hard to believe. I had grown up in Hela Province, among the Huli people, and while we had our own ways of living and solving problems, I had never thought of them as inventions that mattered beyond our valleys. But as I reflected, I began to see connections between what the Chinese had created and what my own people had developed for survival in the Highlands.

I remember sitting in my dormitory room at Tianjin University of Technology and Education, thinking about gunpowder. The Chinese had discovered it over a thousand years ago, changing warfare and celebrations alike with both weapons and fireworks. For us Huli, war was also a reality of life, but we fought with bows, arrows, and spears. Our strength came not from explosives but from courage, discipline, and a deep knowledge of the land.

When we celebrated, we did not light fireworks in the sky, but we beat our kundu drums, sang our war chants, and painted our faces with bright ochres. Different tools, yes, but the same spirit: to fight, to survive, to show who we were.

Another time, I thought about the invention of printing. In China, printing opened knowledge to the world. Ideas, education, and wisdom spread far beyond what one person could hold in memory. In Hela, we did not have printing presses, but we had elders. They were our *living books*. They carried genealogies, land boundaries, and histories in their minds. Through storytelling, they passed that knowledge down, carefully and precisely, so that nothing was forgotten. I realised then that our elders were like the printed scrolls of Hela—each word chosen with care, repeated, and remembered, so the story would never be lost.

Paper itself made me smile. The Chinese had invented it during the Han Dynasty, and it became the foundation of education, literature, and culture.

In Huli life, we had no paper, but we had bark cloth and bilums. The tapa cloth carried meaning in ceremonies, and the bilum, woven by mothers and sisters, was more than a bag. It accompanied us in every stage of life—from cradle to grave. I thought to myself: if paper carried words and knowledge in China, then the bilum carried identity and memory in Hela.

When I learned that China had invented paper money, I could not help but compare it to our own wealth in pigs and kina shells. The Chinese used notes to trade; we used pigs to build relationships. In bride price, in peacemaking, in compensation, pigs spoke louder than any piece of paper. And just as merchants in China valued paper notes, my people valued the gleaming kina shells, worn proudly as necklaces or exchanged in ceremonies.

The mechanical clock was another wonder. The Chinese had used gears and water power to measure time.

For us, time was written in the environment. We rose with the calls of birds at dawn, worked when the sun was high, and rested when it dipped below the ridges. The flowering of plants told us when to plant, and the buzzing of insects told us when the rains were near.

Their clock was made of wheels and gears. Ours was made of sky, clouds, and forest. I began to see how the human mind could create ways to understand the world, whether by building gears or by reading the land carefully.

And then there was the compass. The Chinese used it to navigate oceans and explore new worlds. We Huli had no seas, but we had mountains, ridges, rivers, and valleys. I thought of the countless times I had followed my uncles across ridges and streams, learning the names of every rock, every bend in the river, and every tree that marked the path. We did not carry compasses, but we carried the stories of our land, etched into memory. That was our navigation system. The compass reminded me that guidance could come from tools, but also from knowledge, observation, and experience.

Even something as simple as the toothbrush had its reflection in Huli life. The Chinese had bristle brushes; we had chewing sticks, salt, and charcoal. I laughed remembering how we children used to chew twigs until they frayed and then scrub our teeth with them. Different materials, same intention—to stay clean, to stay healthy, and to stay presentable. I realised that invention is not always about machines—it is about solving problems, small or large, using what you have.

The more I compared, the more I realised that invention is not only about great machines or tools. The Chinese had technology that shaped the world. We Huli had creativity that shaped survival. Our wigmen, with their elaborate headdresses of human hair and bird feathers, were inventors too. They created beauty, identity, and strength out of what the forest gave them. Where China gave the world fireworks and paper, we gave the world a culture of resilience, self-expression, and belonging. Both were creations that mattered. Both were inventions of the human mind and heart.

Living in China helped me see this clearly. It wasn't just about admiring Chinese inventions—it was about recognising the ingenuity of my own people. The Chinese looked to the stars and crafted compasses; we looked to the mountains and crafted memory. The Chinese carved meaning into paper; we carved meaning into story. The inventions may have been different, but the spirit was the same.

I remember feeling a deep pride as I walked through Tianjin and later visited other cities. Seeing machines, buildings, and technology, I thought not only about how China had advanced, but also about the Huli ways I had carried with me. I realised that creativity and intelligence are not bound to one culture. The Huli had their own genius, slow, patient, deeply connected to the land, the community, and the spirit of our people.

I also began to think about the future. Living in China, surrounded by inventions, I felt like I was entering into the future itself. The high-speed trains, the electronic payments, the massive bridges—they all seemed like pieces of tomorrow, but built today. I compared this to Hela, where our rivers, mountains, and gardens also guided the future of our lives, but in a slower, more patient rhythm. I understood that invention can look different in every culture, but the desire to solve problems, to survive, and to create beauty is universal.

Every day, I noticed connections. When Chinese students explained their work, I thought about my uncles building gardens with stone walls, my mother weaving bilums, my elders passing down stories. They were all inventors in their own way. They solved problems, preserved knowledge, and left something for the next generation. That is invention too.

China's inventions taught me that history is alive, that learning is not just about books, but about understanding the world and the people who live in it. I began to see the value in observing carefully, experimenting patiently, and building slowly. It reminded me of Hela, where the land teaches, and the elders guide, and every action carries meaning.

I remember thinking of fireworks and kundu drums together. Both announce presence, both mark celebration. One comes from gunpowder and metal; the other comes from wood, skin, and spirits. Both are invention, both are human creativity. I began to see the world as a place full of inventions waiting to be discovered, not only in machines, but in people, cultures, and traditions.

I felt grateful that I could live in China while carrying Hela with me. I carried both knowledge and wisdom—the inventions of China and the inventions of my own people. I understood that being a Huli woman in China did not make me less part of the modern world; it made me a bridge between two ways of knowing. I could admire rockets and compasses, and also bilums and drumbeats. I could learn from fast trains and electronic money, while still following the mountains and rivers in my memory.

By the end of my first year, I realised I had been carrying two kinds of knowledge: one from my Huli heritage, one from China. Both were valuable. Both were necessary. Both shaped me into a person who could walk between worlds, learn from both, and share that learning with others. I felt proud, strong, and ready for the challenges ahead.

Studying in China had not only taught me about Chinese inventions—it had taught me about the value of my own culture, and how it could stand alongside the rest of the world.

The more I thought about it, the more I understood that invention is everywhere. It is in steel and paper, and it is in gardens and songs. It is in rockets and in bilums. It is in fireworks and in drumbeats. It is in people who take the land, the materials, and the knowledge around them and create something meaningful. China showed me one kind of invention; Hela showed me another. Both gave me courage and pride.

I felt like I had entered a world where past and future met, and I carried Hela within me as I explored it. Every new invention I saw reminded me of the ingenuity of people everywhere. Every new machine, every new technology, every new building was another lesson, another story. And through it all, I felt connected to both places—China and Hela—understanding that the same human spirit flows through every culture, shaping the present and the future.

By the time I returned to my dorm after long days of study and exploration, I often sat quietly, holding my bilum, thinking of my ancestors.

20

LIVING IN A CASHLESS SOCIETY

When I came back into Wuhan in November of 2022, my feet touched the streets like they were old stones of memory, stones I had walked before, and my heart beat with both excitement and fear.

Eleven years had passed since I first came here as a young Huli woman from the mountains of Papua New Guinea, filled with curiosity, fear, and determination.

Back then, Wuhan had been the first Chinese city where I lived, studied, and struggled to adjust. I had cried at night because I missed the mist over my Hela valley, the sound of kundu drums, the smell of sweet potato roasted in hot stones. Yet I had also laughed in classrooms when I finally understood a Chinese phrase, or when I walked the streets with classmates from every corner of the world. I had taken home a bachelor's degree from those years, a gift that changed not only my life but my family's.

And now, stepping again into Wuhan after eleven years, I carried inside me both the old memories and the new hope of a doctorate degree. I looked up at the sky, reached my hand into the cool autumn air, and whispered, "Finally free." The words floated out like smoke from a fire.

The sun was hot that day, stronger than I expected. I was thirsty, and as I walked, I saw a street vendor pushing a trolley stacked with baskets of fruit. The watermelons were large, striped green and black, glistening in the sun. My mouth watered. I waved him over, and he stopped. I pointed to one melon, and he weighed it and told me the price. I reached into my wallet, pulled out a hundred-yuan note, and held it out proudly. I remembered in 2011 how I had paid for everything in cash — coins and notes were like companions, always in my bilum.

But to my surprise, he did not take the cash. He smiled gently and shook his head. He pointed to a laminated card hanging from his cart. On it was a black-and-white square pattern. I looked at it, confused. He pointed again, then showed me his phone. Only then did I realise — he wanted me to scan the QR code.

My hand froze for a moment. I thought of my mother at Koroba market, selling kaukau and bananas, carefully folding each kina note into her blouse. I thought of how she licked her finger before peeling notes apart, how she counted coins into her bilum like counting shells.

And here I was, holding cash in my hand, but no one wanted it. Money was invisible now, living inside a machine. Slowly, I pulled out my phone, opened my WeChat app, scanned the code, and typed in the price. In seconds, it was done. He checked his phone, nodded, and smiled as he handed me the melon. I stood there amazed, holding the fruit heavy in my hands, and whispered, "I felt like I was entering into the future."

It was such a simple act — buying a melon — yet it showed me how much China had changed. In 2011, I had carried jingling coins in my bilum, worried that I might lose them on the bus. Now, in 2022, even a fruit seller refused cash. I had stepped from one world into another.

In the following weeks, I kept seeing the same thing everywhere. On buses, no one dropped coins into boxes anymore. Instead, they tapped their phones or flashed QR codes at a machine that beeped. In the campus canteen, students paid not with small notes but with their phones. In the supermarket, even old grandmothers held phones to pay for rice and vegetables. The sound of cash had disappeared. It was replaced by the sound of beeps and the sight of glowing phone screens.

One day, I even saw a beggar sitting by the roadside. He did not hold out his hand or a tin for coins. Instead, he held a cardboard sign with a printed QR code on it. People passed, scanned it with their phones, and kept walking. My heart sank a little. I thought of beggars back in PNG, who sit outside shops calling softly, "Sista, help mi liklik." There, we drop coins into their hands. Here, even begging had become digital. I stood staring at that sign for a long time, my mind caught between wonder and sadness.

I thought about home. In Hela, the market is a living place. Women sit in lines with kaukau piled in neat heaps, with greens, bananas, peanuts, sugarcane. Buyers come, squat down, ask the price, touch the food, smile or argue. Money is exchanged slowly, deliberately, folded and tucked into a bilum. Sometimes, if someone is short by a kina, the seller still gives the food, saying, "Em orait, yu save mi." Relationships and trust are part of every transaction. Here in Wuhan, the transactions were lightning fast, but faceless. The code did not smile, did not argue, did not forgive. It only beeped.

Yet I could not deny how convenient it was. One evening I walked into a small noodle shop near the university. I ordered Wuhan's famous hot dry noodles. When it came time to pay, I offered cash again, just to test. The owner smiled, shook his head, and pointed to the QR code. I laughed, pulled out my phone, scanned, and instantly the payment was done. I carried my steaming bowl to a table, the sesame paste rich and fragrant. As I ate, I thought of my Huli people, where eating and paying are tied to relationships — you eat, then you return the favour later with food or help. Here, payment was a quick beep, nothing more.

Another day, I needed to take a taxi. In 2011, I would stand on the roadside waving my arm, then hand the driver cash at the end. But now I opened the Didi app on my phone, typed in my destination, and within minutes a car arrived. I climbed in, and when the ride ended, I did not hand over a note. The payment went through automatically on my phone. The driver nodded, and I stepped out. It was so smooth that I almost felt empty, as if something had been skipped. Back home, handing money to a driver is part of the journey. Here, the journey ended with a beep I did not even control.

The more I lived this way, the more I realised I was carrying two worlds inside me. In my bilum, woven by my mother from bush fibers, I now carried only my phone and charger. That bilum once held coins, folded notes, and even tobacco leaves. Now it carried a machine that connected me to banks, shops, taxis, and hospitals. The bilum and the phone, the old and the new, travelled together on my shoulder. Sometimes I imagined them talking to each other quietly: the bilum whispering stories of pigs and shells, the phone whispering codes and signals.

Soon I had to open a Chinese bank account again. In 2011, I had stood in long lines, filling out forms, holding my passport, and waiting as the teller counted out my money. In 2022, the process was quicker. My phone number, my passport, my digital identity were all linked. Money flowed directly into my WeChat and Alipay accounts. I could pay my bills without touching a note. It amazed me, but it also frightened me. What if the system failed? What if I lost my phone? In PNG, if you lose your wallet, you can still find money in the garden, in pigs, in family. Here, if you lose your phone, it feels like losing your whole life.

I saw students around me using their phones for everything — to buy train tickets, to order food, to pay electricity, to send money to family. It became clear that in China, mobile phones were no longer just for calling or chatting. They were wallets, ID cards, tickets, even health passes. I remembered how during COVID-19, China required green health codes on phones to enter buildings. Without a phone, you could not move. This was a new kind of world, one I had to learn quickly to survive in.

I kept comparing it to Hela. At home, we still measure wealth in pigs, shells, and land. A man is rich not because he has money in a bank but because he has pigs in the pen, land for gardens, and family alliances. When I told my relatives about cashless payment, they laughed. One uncle said, "How can you trust money you cannot see? Better I see my pigs with my eyes." I laughed with him, but I also knew the world is moving toward this invisible money, whether we like it or not.

Each day I practiced. I paid for coffee with my phone. I recharged my metro card with my phone. I even sent money to classmates with just a few taps. The more I did it, the more natural it felt. Yet every time, I remembered my mother's hands counting coins. The memory never left me.

As weeks passed, I realised China was not just using WeChat and Alipay. The government was introducing the digital yuan, e-CNY. I read that this would replace even the private apps, giving the central bank more control. It made me think of PNG again. We had only recently welcomed the Bank of China to open in our country. Could PNG one day jump straight into digital currency? Could our mothers and fathers learn to scan codes at Tari market? I tried to imagine my mother holding a smartphone instead of a bilum full of coins. It felt impossible, but I also knew our people learn quickly when there is need.

Sometimes at night, I would walk back to my dormitory, carrying my bilum, the lights of Wuhan glowing around me. Neon signs flickered, QR codes shone from billboards, people hurried past staring at their phones. I would stop and look up, whispering again, "I felt like I was entering into the future." And I knew that my journey here was not just about earning a doctorate. It was about learning how the world was changing and finding a way to bring those lessons back to my people.

Because in Hela, life is still slow, tied to the land, the pigs, the family. But in Wuhan, life runs on codes and signals, invisible yet powerful. My task was to be the bridge between those two worlds, to carry the knowledge as my mother wove the bilum — carefully, patiently, strand by strand, until it is strong.

21

TECHNOLOGY BEYOND IMAGINATION

I never thought my feet would walk on the streets of China. My village, deep in the mountains of Hela, feels far from the world, but somehow, I found myself on a plane, looking down at a land that is all metal and light. Even before I left, people in my village said, "Huli woman, what will you see there?" I could not answer them. I only knew my heart wanted to see, to touch, to feel what I had heard of, what I had dreamed of—China's machines that think, buildings that touch the sky, lights that move like fire in the night.

The first thing I noticed when I arrived was the sound. My village is full of birds, full of river water rushing, full of voices that carry across valleys. Here, in the city, the sound is like a river of metal. Cars, trains, people, and machines—they all make one great humming.

I stood for a long time, looking, feeling. My skin prickled. My heart was curious and afraid at the same time. I remembered the sound of rain in the Hela mountains, how it patters slowly on leaves and soil, how it sings of growth and life. This sound here was not singing. It was shouting, constant, everywhere. And yet, I realised, it too was alive.

I remember the first time I saw a robot. I was in a market, not like our small village markets with sweet potato and pigs. This market was bright and cold, filled with screens and machines. A robot walked towards me, its movements smooth and quick, handing a cup of tea to a man. I stepped back, my hand touching my chest, because I did not know if it was alive. It smiled—or I thought it did, because the screen made a mouth—and I laughed nervously. My mind tried to understand.

In Hela, we have spirits in the forest, and I wondered, "Is this another kind of spirit, or just metal pretending to be a spirit?" I touched the robot lightly, expecting cold, expecting nothing. But I felt something: the intention of humans. Even metal carries care if humans shape it that way.

The trains came next. I had seen trucks and buses in my village, rattling and noisy. But the Chinese trains moved like rivers of silver. They moved so fast I could not see the trees beside the tracks.

I thought of our mountain paths, where my feet carry me slowly, where I have time to see the orchids and the ants, where I can smell the wet earth after rain. Here, I blinked, and the scenery was gone. I wondered, "How do people live with so much speed?" I held onto the rail and felt the rhythm of the train move through my bones. It was strange and exciting, like touching lightning without fear.

Then there were the phones. Oh, the phones. In Hela, a phone is a gift, something we use to call our families far away. Here, every person has a phone that can open doors, pay for food, show maps, even talk to the sky. I watched people move money from hand to hand, or sometimes no hands at all, just a wave of fingers across the screen. My mind spun. In our village, money is yams, pigs, and small green leaves sometimes used for trade. Here in China, it is only light and numbers. I wondered if the trees and rivers understood it. I laughed quietly to myself, imagining trying to trade a yam with a machine.

One night, I walked by a building that was taller than the mountain near my village. Lights shone like hundreds of fireflies frozen in the sky. I touched the wall—it was cold and smooth, not like our stones. I remembered our huts, made of wood, made of the sweat of hands, and I felt a little afraid. A voice inside whispered, "This is power. This is knowledge we do not know yet." And yet, there was beauty too. The lights danced gently in patterns I could not name. I wanted to touch them all, to catch them like fireflies and take them home.

I visited a factory, a place where machines work and humans watch. In our village, we work with our hands and our feet. Here, machines move faster than any human, carrying metal, cutting metal, building metal. I stood and watched a machine paint a car with colours that shone like sunlight on wet leaves. I felt small, but I also felt a strange joy, because humans made this. Our people in Hela make fire from stone, make gardens from soil, make songs from voices. Here, humans make speed from metal, and songs from light. The song is different, but it is still a song.

One evening, I went to a place with water. It was not river water, not mud and stone. It was clean, shining, moving like a glass river, and people rode in small boxes that floated above it. "Maglev," they called it. I held the railing and my stomach jumped with fear and wonder. I thought of our canoes, drifting slowly in the foggy rivers of home. I laughed, because I never thought I would fly in metal, above the water, above the city, moving faster than my eyes could follow. I felt dizzy and alive, a mixture of fear and trust, and I whispered to myself, "May the spirits watch over this journey."

I stayed with a family for a few days. They spoke fast, and I spoke slower. Sometimes we laughed, sometimes we looked at each other in silence. I asked about the machines, the lights, the buildings. They told me, and I tried to understand.

I thought of our elders in Hela, telling stories of ancestors and spirits, of the forest and the river. I told the Chinese family about the mountains I come from, about the pigs and gardens, about the smoke from fires that smelled like home. They listened, and

I knew the world was bigger than my mountains, but maybe also smaller, because we could talk and share.

Food was strange too. I ate noodles that slid down my throat like water, dumplings that hid warmth inside, and fruits I could not name. I tried steamed buns that were soft and smelled like clouds. I bit into them and tasted sweetness I had never known. I walked past markets that smelled of fried dough, sweet pastries, spices I could not name, roasted chestnuts burning on small metal grills. My nose and eyes drank in everything.

In Hela, food comes from the earth or the garden, cooked over fire, smelled in the smoke. Here, food comes from machines, from kitchens of shining steel. I learned to eat, to taste, to enjoy, but I remembered the taste of our sweet potato, the smoky flavour of roasted pork, the fresh bitterness of mountain greens. I carried those tastes in my memory like treasure, placing them gently next to the new flavours I was discovering.

I took a bus one morning that had no driver. I watched as it moved, slow at first, then faster, stopping exactly where it should. People got on and off. I touched my heart. I thought, "If I could ride this in Hela, maybe I would never be afraid of the mountains, maybe I would see the forests in one long breath." But then I laughed, because I knew our mountains would not let metal move like this. The land has its own rules, and machines must learn them too.

Everywhere I went, I saw cameras, screens, lights, machines. I thought of our spirits watching the forest, the winds telling the trees stories. Here, humans watch each other and the machines watch humans. I was not sure if it was good or bad. I was only sure it was different. And I was learning to walk in a different world, to breathe in its speed, to touch its metal, to laugh at its fire that was not fire.

Sometimes I sat quietly and imagined my village. I imagined my mother carrying sweet potatoes, my father carving wood, the children running through mud. And then I looked around, and I saw people carrying phones, machines building, lights moving, rivers of steel flowing, and I thought, "The world is big. The heart must be big too." I realised that my heart had grown, stretching beyond mountains and rivers, embracing the new, holding the old, carrying both in the same beat.

One day, I went to a museum of the future. They showed things I could not imagine: cars that flew, machines that made other machines, lights that drew pictures in the air. I touched them with my fingers, careful not to break them, careful not to break myself. I remembered the first time I touched a river in Hela, the first time I felt rain on my bare feet. The feeling was not the same, but it was alive. It was a new kind of life; a life made from human hands and minds.

I kept walking, every day, learning. I learned that technology is like the forest: it grows, it reaches, it changes. I learned that speed is not always good, and that stillness is always needed. I learned that people, no matter where, are people: laughing, crying, afraid, brave. And I learned that a Hela woman can walk in the metal forests of China and still carry the soil of home in her heart.

After a few days, I took a walk along a street that was lined with hundreds of tiny shops. Each one smelled different: roasted peanuts, sweet dumplings, strange herbs that burned my nose, smoke from tiny charcoal fires, incense from temples tucked in between the buildings.

I stopped at a little stall where a man sold steamed buns with red bean filling. The dough was soft as clouds, and I could feel the warmth through my fingers before I bit into it. The sweetness touched my tongue, and I thought of the wild honey we gather in the mountains, the taste of sugarcane, the fruit we pick from hidden trees. Somehow, this city flavour and the forest flavour mixed in my mouth, and I laughed softly at the strange, beautiful mix.

One afternoon, I found a small temple hidden between two tall buildings. Smoke curled up from a clay pot, curling and twisting like the smoke from our village fires. I knelt and watched people place coins, bow their heads, whisper prayers. I touched the cool stone walls and whispered my own prayer: "Guide me, spirit of machines, spirit of mountains, spirit of sky." In Hela, spirits are everywhere—in trees, rivers, wind, fire. Here, I realised, humans carry their own spirits in stone and metal, in light and ritual. And maybe the machine and the spirit are not enemies. Maybe they can speak to each other through humans.

The metro fascinated me more every day. It moved silently beneath the city, carrying thousands like ants through tunnels of steel. I pressed my hand against the cool railing, thinking of the mountains of Hela, and I imagined if our people could ride through tunnels like this. They would laugh with fear and wonder, clinging to each other, smelling the cool air that carried stories from faraway places. The metro was fast, precise, unafraid. And yet, I thought of the forest paths, uneven and slow, full of life, full of danger, full of beauty. Both teach patience, just in different ways.

One evening, I wandered into a small street filled with lights that blinked in colours I could not name. The air smelled of fried food and something sweet, spicy, unfamiliar. Children ran laughing, chasing bubbles from a small machine that blew them endlessly. I watched a boy and a girl fight over a bubble that shimmered in pink and gold light. I thought of our children in Hela, running through mud, catching frogs, throwing sticks into rivers. Different lands, different bubbles, but the same joy. I laughed quietly, remembering my own childhood, the warmth of fire on my back, the taste of roasted yams, the wind in my hair.

I also visited a school for children learning coding and robotics. Their hands were small, precise, careful. I watched a little girl teach a robot to dance. It moved jerkily at first, then smooth, then perfectly synchronised with music that no one could hear but the machines understood. I clapped, and the children laughed, because they understood the joy I felt. Joy is the same everywhere. It does not matter if it comes from drums, birds, a child's song, or a machine's dance. I felt warmth in my chest, remembering the songs of my ancestors, the drums that called us to dance, the fire that lit our nights.

I visited a hospital where machines helped heal people. Robots measured temperature, delivered medicine, scanned bodies, assisted surgeons. I held my hands together and whispered, "Guide them, spirits of light, spirits of metal, spirits of hands." In Hela, healing comes from herbs, from fire, from touch, from prayer. Here, humans use the hands of machines. And yet, the care is the same. People want to heal, to live, to be safe. The tools may change, but the human heart does not.

One day, I climbed a tall tower and looked out over the city. Roads flowed like silver rivers, lights blinked like stars fallen to earth, trains zipped like metal snakes, and the river reflected them all. I closed my eyes and imagined our mountains: mist curling over trees, fireflies glowing, children laughing, rivers moving slowly over stones. When I opened my eyes, I saw the city, all metal and light, fast and alive. And I realised my heart could hold both: the forest and the city, the mud and the concrete, the fire and the lights. Both are alive, both have lessons, both have spirit.

I went to a laboratory where rockets and satellites were built. I touched a model of a small satellite and whispered, "Fly far, see far, guide humans carefully." In Hela, we watch the stars for planting, for hunting, for life. Here, humans reach for the stars with machines. Different ways, same desire: to know, to explore, to live better. I felt pride in humans everywhere, whether carrying yams through mud or satellites through the sky.

I walked through a street market late at night. The smells were overwhelming—roasted chestnuts, fried dough, spicy meats, sweet fruits I could not name. A small cart sold fried insects. I watched children pick them with delight, crunching loudly. I laughed quietly. In Hela, we eat worms and insects sometimes, roasted over fire, children laughing as they dare each other to eat more. Somehow, across the world, children are the same. The laughter, the daring, the joy—it is universal.

I visited a technology exhibition where machines painted pictures, composed music, and even wrote poems. I put my hand to a small robot, and it moved, responding to my touch. It wrote a poem about the mountains, though it did not know Hela. I read it and laughed softly. Machines can imitate, but humans feel. Humans feel the rain on their skin, the warmth of a fire, the smell of earth, the laughter of children. Machines can learn, but humans live. I understood then that the future is not just metal and light. The future is the dance of human spirit with machines.

Eventually, I returned to my village, carrying stories, memories, lessons, and flavours of distant lands. I told the children about machines that fly, trains that move like rivers, robots that dance, hospitals where machines heal. I told them about cities of light, people moving fast but still loving, machines helping humans reach farther than ever before. They listened with wide eyes. I saw in them the same curiosity that carried me across the world.

But I also told them about home. About soil, fire, smoke, rivers, mountains. I told them that even in a world of machines, we carry the earth in our hands, the spirit in our hearts. I told them to learn, to explore, to see the world, but never to forget the lessons of home. The mountains teach patience. The rivers teach care. The soil teaches life. And the heart teaches all else.

I learned that technology is not the enemy. It is a tool, a partner, a teacher. It can move faster than mountains, see farther than eyes, heal deeper than hands.

But it cannot love, it cannot sing, it cannot smell rain, it cannot feel the soil beneath its feet. That is the gift we carry from our ancestors, from our mountains, from our rivers. That is why a Hela woman can walk in China, touch machines that think, fly in trains faster than the wind, and still feel home.

I understood that the world is big, full of light and metal, full of fire and smoke. It is full of people trying, learning, caring. It is full of joy, fear, love, laughter, curiosity. And I realised that a human heart can hold both: the forest of Hela, with its slow, patient rhythm, and the city of China, with its fast, bright, humming energy.

Both are alive, both are important, and both teach the same lesson: to live, to learn, to love, to move forward, and to remember where we come from.

I carry this story with me, every day. The machines, the lights, the cities, the rivers, the robots, the hospitals, the markets—they all live in my memory. But so do the mountains, the fire, the rivers, the smoke, the songs of my people. And when I close my eyes, I can walk both worlds. I can feel the hum of metal and the beat of drums. I can hear the voice of the city and the song of the forest. I can see the lights and the stars. I can touch machines and soil. I can be a Hela woman, and a citizen of the world.

And that is my lesson: the world moves fast, but the heart moves faster. Machines can teach, cities can dazzle, lights can blind. But the spirit, the soul, the care, the love we carry inside— that is our guide. That is what makes us human. That is what makes us alive. That is what I learned, walking through China, touching the future, carrying home in my heart.

PART IV

TRANSFORMATION AND RETURN

22

A NEW ME

When I first arrived in China, I carried more than luggage; I carried my life in a bilum, woven with the threads of Hela, of the mountains and valleys where I grew up, of the songs and stories my elders told by the fire.

I had expectations, yes, but also doubts. Would I belong in this place so far from home, so full of noise, lights, and people speaking languages I barely understood? I remember pressing my forehead to the airplane window as we descended, trying to memorise the outline of the cities below, the rivers, the buildings, the streets stretching into the horizon, and I thought to myself, "This is where my future begins, but will I still know who I am?"

In those first weeks, I felt small. I walked through universities with students who seemed confident, fluent, and knowledgeable. Their pens moved quickly, their voices clear in discussion, their hands swiping across phones as if they controlled time itself. I clutched my bilum, feeling the weight of my ancestors, the weight of expectations from my family back in Hela, and the weight of my own ambition. I realised immediately that studying in China would not only challenge my intellect but also challenge my understanding of myself.

Back home, identity had always been simple in some ways. I was Huli, daughter of my clan, raised to respect the land, my elders, and the traditions that shaped daily life. I knew the songs, the dances, the rituals. I knew my responsibilities: to learn, to help, to carry the memory of those who came before me. But in China, I was not just Huli. I was also a student, a foreigner, a woman in a world that sometimes seemed to move faster than I could follow. My identity stretched in ways it had never stretched before. I learned quickly that being Huli did not mean being static—it meant being rooted, yes, but also growing outward, learning new ways to stand, walk, and speak.

The first shift in my mindset came through education itself. In Hela, learning was often guided by elders, stories, and memory. In China, learning demanded questioning, curiosity, and reflection. Professors expected more than memorisation; they wanted understanding, insight, and creativity. I remember sitting in my first lecture, struggling to follow, my mind leaping from words to concepts, trying to connect what I knew of my world with what was being taught. I had to remind myself to breathe, to write slowly, to trust that I could absorb these new ideas without losing the foundation I carried from Hela. It was exhausting at first, but with each day, I felt my mind stretching, growing, and opening.

Language, too, reshaped my identity. Mandarin was not just a tool to speak; it became a lens to see the world differently. At first, the tones, the characters, and the flow of conversation felt like a river too swift to cross. But as I practiced, stumbled, and tried again, I discovered that speaking another language changed how I thought, how I perceived ideas, and how I approached problems. I realised that identity is not fixed; it can expand to include new ways of seeing, new ways of being, without losing the core of who you are. My Huli identity, far from being diminished, grew richer. I was not just Huli in body; I was Huli in conversation, in reflection, and in the way I connected with a world far from my mountains.

Living in a city like Wuhan or Shanghai reshaped my sense of scale and possibility. In Hela, the tallest structures were the ridges and the men's houses. Here, towers rose above the clouds, trains glided through the sky, and driverless cars moved silently through streets filled with people. At first, I felt small and uncertain. How could I, from a small village, stand in the shadow of this new world and still hold my voice? Slowly, I began to understand that my smallness was not weakness; it was perspective. I could observe, learn, and take the lessons of a city that seemed impossible and translate them into my life, back home or wherever I would go next. The mountains of Hela taught endurance; the streets of China taught efficiency. Together, they reshaped my vision of what it meant to grow, to lead, and to create.

I noticed the change in my daily habits. I woke earlier, organised my day, and planned tasks with a discipline I had never needed at home. I learned to manage time precisely, to balance study, work, and rest. In Hela, time was measured by the sun, the harvest, the drums. In China, it was measured in minutes, appointments, and schedules. Both are valid, I realised, but combining them gave me strength. I learned to be flexible, patient, and proactive. I began to see that mindset is not just about thinking; it is about organising oneself, choosing what to focus on, and acting deliberately.

Friendships also reshaped my sense of self. I met students from Africa, Europe, and all over Asia. Some shared languages, others shared stories of resilience. I learned to communicate across differences, to listen deeply, to find connection in gestures, smiles, and shared meals. In Hela, community is intimate, born of shared land and ancestry. Here, community was chosen, negotiated, and built across cultures. I learned that belonging is not just about geography; it is about engagement, understanding, and mutual respect.

Technology became another teacher. I had seen driverless cars, skytrains, QR code payments, AI-powered education tools, and robots in restaurants. At first, it felt alien, almost unreal. But I realised that technology is not just about convenience—it is about possibility. It taught me that the future is not something to wait for; it is something we must step into, create, and understand. And when I compared it to the ingenuity of my own people in Hela—our bilums, our gardens, our intricate dances—I saw the same principle at work: creativity solves problems, connects people, and shapes the world. My mindset shifted from seeing limitations to seeing potential, from measuring success only in certificates to measuring it in curiosity, skill, and vision.

I began to reflect deeply on ambition. In Hela, ambition is often quiet, expressed in skill, leadership, and responsibility. In China, ambition is visible, celebrated, and driven by results. Observing both, I realised that ambition is not about erasing culture or self; it is about expanding horizons while carrying identity intact. I learned to dream larger, to imagine my future as a blend of Huli wisdom and global knowledge, of ancestral memory and modern innovation.

Each research paper I wrote, every class discussion I participated in, every cultural misunderstanding I navigated, shaped me. I learned patience, humility, and resilience. I learned that mistakes are not failure—they are lessons, and growth is built on them. I realised that identity is layered. Being Huli does not prevent me from being a student of the world. Being a student of the world does not erase my Huli roots. Instead, these layers make me stronger, more adaptable, and more aware of my place in the wider story of humanity.

By the time my first year ended, I felt a new confidence. I walked the streets of Wuhan differently. I approached my studies with focus, but also curiosity. I spoke with professors and peers, often stumbling in language but never in spirit. I began mentoring younger students from PNG, sharing tips, comfort, and encouragement. In teaching them, I realised that knowledge is not just personal—it is a bridge between worlds. I could carry my experience, my growth, and my vision back to my homeland, and perhaps inspire others to see that identity is not a cage; it is a foundation.

I started keeping a journal, noting changes in myself, moments of insight, and reflections on culture. I wrote about walking under neon lights, riding driverless cars, and seeing rivers of people flowing across bridges. I wrote about the sounds of my Hela home—the kundu drums, birds, smoke of cooking fires—and how they lived within me even here, in a city that seemed so different. I began to notice the subtle ways my thinking had shifted: I could organise, analyse, question, and create in ways that felt new, yet deeply connected to the wisdom I had carried all my life.

One night, as I sat looking at the skyline from my dormitory window, I realised that the "new me" was not someone leaving Hela behind. She was a woman who could carry Hela in her heart while embracing the world. She was patient yet ambitious, humble yet confident, rooted yet open. I felt a vision forming—not just of my future career, but of the life I wanted to build: a life that bridges worlds, a life that honours my ancestors while shaping a path forward for those who come after me.

Studying in China taught me that identity is fluid, mindset is powerful, and vision is essential. I saw that the future does not come passively; it is created by those who act, reflect, and learn continuously. I realised that success is not only about degrees, money, or status—it is about self-understanding, integrity, and the courage to step into the unknown.

I began dreaming bigger dreams. I imagined programs in PNG inspired by what I had seen: education integrating technology with culture, leadership rooted in identity but open to global ideas, communities that balance tradition and innovation. I imagined mentoring girls from Hela, showing them that being a daughter of the mountains does not limit their potential; it gives them strength to reach farther than they imagined.

By the time my final year approached, I saw a complete shift in myself. I could walk into a lecture hall with confidence, speak to professors with clarity, navigate the city independently, and mentor others across cultures. I had learned to turn uncertainty into curiosity, fear into courage, and observation into strategy. I had grown into a person who could live in two worlds at once: the world of my roots and the world of endless possibilities.

I pressed my bilum close one evening, remembering my mother's words when I left Hela: "Carry us with you, no matter where you go." I understood now that carrying my people did not mean staying the same—it meant growing responsibly, learning courageously, and returning enriched. My identity was not lost in China; it was expanded, strengthened, and made luminous by experience.

In classrooms, libraries, and the streets of Wuhan, I saw that knowledge is not a destination—it is a journey. And that journey reshapes the traveller. I was no longer the timid girl from Hela; I was a woman who could navigate the future while honouring the past. I could see challenges clearly, find solutions, and dream of what was possible. I had learned that mindset shapes reality, that identity shapes choice, and that vision shapes destiny.

As I prepared to graduate, I realised that this chapter of my life in China had given me more than education. It had given me self-awareness, resilience, and hope. I had learned that being Huli is a strength, not a limitation, and that the world, as vast as it is, has a place for women like me who carry both roots and wings. I had grown into a new me, a woman who can step forward into tomorrow with purpose, clarity, and pride.

Every time I think of the journey, I see the skyline of Wuhan, the neon lights reflecting in the river, the quiet hum of driverless cars, the soaring skytrains, and I feel a deep, quiet joy. That city, with its challenges and lessons, reshaped me. It taught me patience, courage, and vision. It taught me that identity is not only inherited; it is also created, lived, and renewed. It taught me that the new me is not separate from Hela; she is Hela grown outward, shining into the world.

And so, as I take the next step in my life, I carry both home and the world within me. I am no longer just a student; I am a bridge, a learner, a dreamer, and a woman ready to create the future while honouring the past. I feel the pulse of possibility in my veins, the rhythm of my ancestors in my heart, and the promise of a life fully lived in my mind. This is the new me: a Huli woman with the courage to enter the future, grounded in heritage, but open to all that life offers.

23

LESSONS FOR PAPUA NEW GUINEA

I was born in a small valley in Papua New Guinea, where the mountains rise like guardians and the rivers sing endlessly to themselves. My earliest memories are not of big cities or tall buildings, but of the smell of earth after rain, the creak of bamboo walls in the wind, and the laughter of children running barefoot along muddy tracks.

Life in the village was simple, yet heavy with struggle. My mother carried bilums full of kaukau on her back, walking for hours just to sell them at the market. My father's hands were calloused from cutting firewood and digging gardens, yet he still smiled when he saw us waiting for him in the evenings.

We lived with hope, though the world beyond our valley often felt impossibly far. The nearest road was rough and unreliable. Trucks rarely came, and when they did, they demanded high fees that we could not always pay. To reach the nearest health center, we walked for hours. I still remember the cries of a neighbour's wife who lost her baby because the clinic was too far and no vehicle came in time. Even as a child, I wondered why promises of government help never seemed to reach us. I heard my parents talk about leaders in Port Moresby and the speeches they made on the radio, full of talk about development and modernity. But those words floated in the air like smoke, never landing in our village.

As I grew older, I became curious about the wider world. At school, though our classrooms had broken windows and our books were often missing pages, I discovered stories of other nations. Some seemed impossibly distant, with their trains, skyscrapers, and electricity lighting up entire landscapes. Among them, China fascinated me most. Our teachers told us that once, not so long ago, China had been poor too, filled with villages not unlike ours, where people tilled the soil and struggled with hunger. For many years, the world looked down on China, calling it backward. Yet somehow, in just a few decades, it transformed itself into one of the most powerful nations on earth.

The first time I saw a documentary about China's cities, I was astonished. Trains moved so fast they blurred, bridges stretched like ribbons across valleys, and whole cities glowed with lights at night. Factories buzzed, farmers sold their produce in modern markets, and students studied in universities that seemed larger than some of our towns. It made me wonder: if China could rise from such hardship, why not us? Why not Papua New Guinea?

Years later, when I had the chance to travel to Beijing as part of a women exchange program, those questions returned to me with even greater force. We landed at night, and as the plane descended, I pressed my face against the window. The city spread below like a sea of stars. Lights traced the lines of highways, towers rose like candles in the dark, and I felt at once small and hopeful. Over the next weeks, we travelled to different provinces, meeting women, farmers, and entrepreneurs. What struck me most was not only the wealth of the cities but the transformation of the villages. Roads wound through mountains that once seemed impassable. Farmers spoke proudly of selling their produce online. Children in rural schools carried tablets in their hands, learning not just to read and write but to use technology to connect with the wider world.

I thought constantly of home. I thought of my village, where even a blackboard was sometimes missing from our school, and of the farmers who sold their coffee at prices so low they could barely buy salt. I thought of my mother, who carried bilums heavy with food yet earned only a few kina at the market. In those moments, I realised that China's story was not just a distant tale. It was a mirror, showing us what might be possible if only we dared to learn, to plan, and to change.

The first lesson that impressed me was vision. In conversations with Chinese hosts, I heard over and over about the importance of long-term planning. They spoke of their five-year plans, of how every part of their country's development was guided by a shared national vision. I was struck by the consistency: leaders changed, but the goals remained. It was like planting a tree and tending it year after year, even if the one who planted it might not live to enjoy its full shade.

Back in PNG, I thought about how often our leaders spoke of visions but failed to carry them through. Vision 2050 was meant to guide us into the future, but too often it feels like a book left on a dusty shelf, opened only during speeches. In my own lifetime, I have watched governments change, each one bringing new promises, abandoning old ones, leaving half-built projects behind like skeletons of wasted hope. It is as if we keep planting seeds but never water them long enough to grow. From China I learned that development requires patience, discipline, and above all, continuity.

Another lesson was about roads—simple, ordinary roads that mean everything to those of us who have grown up without them. In China, there is a saying: "To get rich, first build roads." I saw with my own eyes what this meant. In Lanzhou province, once one of the poorest areas, bridges now stretched across valleys so deep they took my breath away. Roads connected farmers to markets, children to schools, and patients to hospitals.

I met a woman who told me that before the roads, it took her two days to walk to the nearest town. Now she could take a bus in less than an hour, selling her produce for far higher prices.

I thought again of my own valley, where villagers carry sick relatives on stretchers for hours to reach clinics, where farmers lose their produce because trucks cannot reach them, where life remains bound by mud tracks and rivers without bridges. We cannot speak of development in PNG if we do not first connect our people. Roads, electricity, and internet are not luxuries; they are lifelines. China showed me that infrastructure is the backbone upon which everything else is built. Without it, we remain scattered islands in the same sea, unable to reach one another.

Education, too, left a deep impression on me. In rural China, I walked into classrooms buzzing with children, their eyes bright, their hands eager. Even in villages, schools were equipped, teachers were supported, and students were encouraged to dream beyond their boundaries. I thought of my own schooling in PNG—sitting on rough benches, sharing tattered books, watching bright classmates drop out because their parents could not afford fees or because teachers had stopped showing up. It broke my heart to see how much potential we lose every year, not because our children lack intelligence, but because our system fails them.

In China, education is more than schooling; it is nation-building. Respect for learning runs deep in their history, from ancient examinations to modern universities. It is this respect that fuels their innovation, their industries, their technology.

I returned home convinced that if PNG truly wants to rise, we must treat education not as charity but as survival. Every kina spent on schools, teachers, and skills is an investment in the future. We must prepare our children not only for white-collar jobs but for industries in agriculture, fisheries, technology, and beyond. Imagine vocational schools in every province, teaching young people how to process coffee, manage tourism, or repair machinery. Education must connect directly to opportunity, giving our young people the tools to shape the economy rather than drift aimlessly.

One of the most inspiring things I witnessed in China was the transformation of rural life. In villages once as poor as ours, people now thrive. Farmers sell their goods online through platforms like Taobao. Entire communities have built new industries, from crafts to specialty foods, finding markets far beyond their borders. Poverty has not disappeared, but it has retreated dramatically, driven back by deliberate policies that focused on the rural majority.

I could not stop thinking of my village. I could see my mother's face as she counted coins after selling kaukau. I could see farmers in the Highlands struggling to sell coffee for fair prices. I imagined what would happen if PNG invested in its villages the way China did—if roads, electricity, and internet brought opportunities directly to our rural people. What if a woman in Gulf Province could sell her fish online? What if a cocoa farmer in Bougainville could connect directly with international buyers? What if a child in Telefomin could study online alongside children in Port Moresby? Development must begin where the majority live—in the village. Otherwise, it will never be real.

Yet no lesson struck me harder than governance and discipline. In China, I saw a nation that, for all its size, moved with purpose. I read about their anti-corruption campaigns, how powerful officials were punished, how the message was clear: corruption destroys development.

In PNG, corruption is the sickness that eats us from within. I have seen it with my own eyes—funds for schools vanishing, health centers left unfinished, roads built poorly because money was siphoned away. Our leaders speak of fighting corruption, but too often the fight ends in silence.

From China I learned that discipline is not only for leaders but for all citizens. It is in how we work, how we use time, how we honour commitments. In PNG, projects stretch on for years, wasting money and hope. In China, projects are completed with speed and precision. We must learn that discipline is not foreign to us; it is a choice we can make, rooted in respect for ourselves and our people.

Technology opened my eyes as well. In Shenzhen, I walked through markets filled with drones, phones, and devices I had never seen before. It was hard to believe that only a few decades ago, the same place was a fishing village. Today it hums with energy, home to companies known worldwide. What struck me was not only the technology but the spirit of the young people who created it. They were bold, inventive, and unafraid to try.

I thought of PNG's youth, full of creativity and energy. With the right support, they too could build, innovate, and leap forward. Mobile phones already connect our villages in ways unthinkable a decade ago. If we embrace technology, we can leapfrog stages of development, creating opportunities in e-commerce, mobile banking, renewable energy, and more. Technology can connect farmers to markets, students to lessons, and communities to knowledge. It is not a luxury; it is a tool of empowerment.

But perhaps the most beautiful lesson from China was about culture. Despite modernisation, China never abandoned its identity. It still celebrates its festivals, its philosophies, its arts. Its culture has become a source of pride and influence, shared across the world. I reflected on our own culture—our 800 languages, our dances, our bilums, our carvings, our *singsings*. We are one of the most diverse nations on earth, yet too often we treat our culture as something to hide rather than celebrate.

I believe development must walk hand in hand with cultural pride. Our traditions are not obstacles; they are assets. Tourism, crafts, music, and storytelling can all be woven into our economy. More than that, culture gives us identity and unity. In a nation as diverse as PNG, we must remind ourselves that we are many but we are one. Just as China draws strength from its heritage, so must we.

As I look back on these lessons, I realise they are not distant theories. They are alive in the stories of ordinary people, both in China and in Papua New Guinea. A woman farmer in Lanzhou selling vegetables online. A mother in my village carrying a bilum full of kaukau. Both seek the same thing: dignity, opportunity, and hope. The difference is that one has been given the tools to rise, while the other still waits.

I am just one woman, born in a valley far from the capital, raised on gardens and rivers. But I carry within me the voices of many Papua New Guineans who dream of a better life. I have seen with my own eyes what is possible. I believe we can rise, if we learn, if we adapt, if we unite. Our story is still being written, and the pen is in our hands.

When I walk through Port Moresby and see cranes building towers, or when I return to my village and watch children run barefoot along dusty tracks, I ask myself: what kind of country will we leave them? Will it be a nation forever caught in promises and poverty, or a nation that, like China, rose against all odds? I believe it can be the latter. I believe Papua New Guinea can stand tall. But we must begin now, with vision, discipline, and pride in who we are.

If China could transform itself in less than a lifetime, then so can we. The road is long, but every journey begins with a single step. And perhaps the first step is this: to believe that we, too, can rise.

24

GIVING BACK – THE DREAM CONTINUES

When I returned from China, I thought the mountains of Hela would greet me the same way they always had. The mist curling over the ridges, the smell of damp soil, the sound of children running barefoot in the mud—all of it was unchanged. But when I stood there, breathing in the smoke of the first fire I lit with my sisters, I felt something different. The mountains were the same, but my eyes had changed. My heart had grown larger. My spirit carried both the soil of my ancestors and the light of the cities I had walked far away from home.

I knew then that I could not keep what I had seen locked inside me. Stories are like rivers: if they are dammed, they stagnate; if they flow, they nourish the land. The stories I brought back from China—about machines that healed, trains that flew like birds, towers that touched the clouds—were not mine to keep. They belonged to the children of my land, especially the girls, who so often are told to stay small, to remain hidden in gardens and kitchens, their voices hushed.

The first time I stood before a classroom in Tari, my knees trembled more than they had in China. Rows of girls sat on benches, their uniforms worn thin, their eyes full of curiosity and doubt. I saw myself in them—bare feet, tired from carrying firewood, hungry for more than just kaukau to fill the stomach. I told them about walking into hospitals where robots carried medicine, about classrooms where girls and boys learned side

197

by side, about a little girl who taught a machine to dance. Their mouths opened wide. Some giggled, others whispered to their friends, "Is it true? Can such things exist?"

I smiled because I remembered asking the same questions when I first saw them. "Yes," I told them. "It is true. These things are real. I touched them with my own hands. And if I could see them, so can you. If I could walk there, so can you. If I could learn, so can you. The only difference between me and you is that I have already gone. But one day, you will go farther than I ever did—if you believe."

The girls stared at me, and in their eyes, I saw the first spark of fire.

At night, I told my own sisters about the children in China. I told them about the way they coded machines with their tiny fingers, about the way they dreamed of reaching the stars. My sisters listened quietly, the flames dancing in their eyes. "Mekeme," the youngest whispered in my Huli name, "I want to go too. I want to see what you saw." Tears filled my eyes. That was all I needed: for them to believe they could.

I carried my stories from school to school, village to village. Sometimes I walked for hours over muddy tracks, the bilum heavy on my back, my voice hoarse by the end of the day. Sometimes I was met with laughter. Some boys scoffed, "What use are your stories? We need jobs, not dreams. We need roads, not robots." I nodded, because their hunger was real. But I told them, "Dreams are the seeds of roads, the seeds of jobs. If you stop dreaming, you stop planting. If you stop planting, nothing will grow."

Some elders frowned and said, "You are filling the children's heads with nonsense. Let them stay where they belong." I bowed my head to them out of respect, but I answered softly, "Our ancestors once thought it was nonsense to make fire from stone. They thought it was madness to climb the highest ridges.

Yet they did. If they had not, we would not stand here today. Do not cut down the path before the children have even taken their first step."

I spoke most fiercely to the girls. "Do not be afraid to be different. When people laugh at you, let their laughter push you forward like the wind fills a bird's wings. When people tell you that you are too small, stand taller, because mountains are made of small stones. When people tell you the world is too big, remember me, a Huli woman, who walked under skyscrapers and came home with the stars in her eyes."

Some lowered their eyes in shyness, some blushed, but I knew my words had gone into them like rain into soil. Seeds do not grow in a day. But I trusted they would grow.

One afternoon, after a talk, a girl followed me quietly down the path. Her uniform was torn, her hair tied in a rough bun, but her eyes burned bright. "Aunty," she whispered, "I want to be like you. But I am poor. My family cannot pay for me to travel. Maybe my dream will die here."

I stopped and held her shoulder. "Child," I said, "poverty is heavy, yes. It bends your back, it closes doors. But it cannot close your mind. It cannot chain your dream. Your dream must be stronger than your hunger, louder than your pain. If you keep walking, if you refuse to give up, the world will make a way. I was once like you, with nothing but the mountains at my back. Yet I walked in China. You can too."

Tears filled her eyes, but she nodded. That nod was a victory greater than any applause.

I also spoke to boys, for they too must change. I told them, "Do not fear strong girls. Do not silence them. When your sister rises, she lifts you too. When a girl learns, the whole village learns. Her strength is not your weakness—it is your wings."

Some shifted uncomfortably, but others listened. Seeds again.

I spoke to mothers weaving bilums under the banana trees.

I told them, "If you give your daughters to the soil only, they will feed your stomach for a while. But if you give them to education, they will feed the nation for generations." Some looked doubtful, some thoughtful, but one or two nodded. Even one nod is the beginning of a river.

I spoke to church gatherings. "God gave us hands to work, minds to think, hearts to love. Do not fear knowledge. Do not fear machines. The danger is not in technology—it is in forgetting compassion. Teach your children to carry both faith and knowledge, both soil and light."

I remembered the discipline I saw in China. People woke early, worked late, dreamed big, moved together. Women drove buses, led companies, built machines. Children learned science without fear. I carried that image home like a torch. I held it high for our youth to see.

"Will you rise?" I asked them. "Will you stop at the garden's edge, or will you step onto the road? Will you let fear chain you, or will you break the chain? The dream continues only if you walk."

In the months that followed, I began to notice changes. A girl once too shy to speak raised her hand in class. A boy who once laughed at books now carried one in his bilum. A parent who once pulled her daughter out of school now let her return. Small things, but rivers grow from drops.

Sometimes, when I was weary, I walked to the river. I sat on the stones, listening to the water's patient song. I thought of the lights of China, rushing, humming, bright. I thought of the river of Hela, slow, steady, eternal. I realised then: both are needed. The fast and the slow. The bright and the dark. The machine and the soil. The youth must learn to carry both in their hands.

I told them, "Do not reject the old. Do not fear the new. Carry your ancestors in one hand, the future in the other. That is how you will stand strong in the world."

And when I finished speaking, I always left them with this: "The dream is not mine alone. It is yours now. It is the dream of your children, and their children. Do not let it die. Carry it like a fire in your bilum. Feed it, guard it, live it. And one day, you will tell your own stories to those who come after you. The dream will continue through you."

This is what China gave me—not only visions of machines and lights, but courage, discipline, unity, belief. This is what I give back to my people, to the youth, to the girls whose voices tremble, to the boys who must learn to walk beside them.

The dream continues. It must continue. It will continue, as long as we keep walking forward, hand in hand, heart to heart, generation to generation.

25

JOURNEY BETWEEN WORLDS (EPILOGUE)

When I think back to where this journey began, my mind does not first go to the great towers of Beijing or the wide bridges of Wuhan. It goes back to the ridges of Hela, to the cold mist lying low on the valley, to the smell of damp earth after rain, to the sound of pigs grunting as they forage near the gardens.

That is where the roots of my life are buried. I am a daughter of the highlands, born into a world of mountains and stories, where knowledge was passed by word of mouth, where a bilum carried both kaukau and dreams, and where the measure of a woman's worth was her strength to endure and to nurture. Yet as I sit here, years later, writing these final words of my story in China, I realise that I have travelled farther than my ancestors ever imagined — not just across geography, but across the invisible spaces of identity, of vision, of *being*.

This journey has been one of crossing worlds, but also of weaving them together. China has not erased who I am as a Huli woman. Instead, it has sharpened me, pulled me apart and stitched me back together with threads I did not know existed.

I arrived carrying the soil of my land in my memory, and I leave carrying the pulse of another land in my bones. To walk between worlds is not easy; it is to constantly be reminded of what you are not, and also of what you might become. But it is also to discover that the self is not a fixed thing. It can stretch.

It can carry both the mist of the mountains and the neon of the cities.

There were days in Wuhan when I stood at a train platform, surrounded by rushing bodies, screens flashing above me, machines beeping at every corner, and I felt like a child again — small, confused, almost invisible. The language swirled around me like a storm, characters I could not catch, words slipping through my ears without meaning. And I would clutch my bilum, my one piece of home, and whisper quietly, "You are still here." In those moments, I thought of my mother's voice, teaching me patience as she planted kaukau in straight rows, saying that life itself grows when you learn to wait. Slowly, I realised that being in China was not about losing myself, but about learning to hold on to the center of me even as the world spun in directions I could not predict.

But there were also days of wonder so great that I could hardly breathe. The first time I rode the skytrain and watched the city spread beneath me like a living map, I thought, "This is the future, and I am inside it." The first time I sat in a driverless car, I whispered a prayer not out of fear, but out of awe, because I felt I was seeing what the world would look like decades from now, and somehow my own feet had carried me into it ahead of time. And then, in the quiet moments after, I thought of the dirt roads of Hela, of the long treks we still make to fetch water or firewood, and I felt both sorrow and determination. To see the future is not only a privilege; it is a responsibility.

In China I learned that progress is not a mystery. It is not a gift that falls from the sky. It is built, stone by stone, line of code by line of code, train by train. It is the work of minds that dare to imagine beyond what is comfortable. And that realisation shifted something deep within me. For so long, my world was framed by survival — by the strength of the body, the endurance of the spirit, the cycles of planting and harvesting, of giving and enduring. China showed me another frame: that the mind, when disciplined and daring, can change not just one life but the course of a nation.

At night, when the city lights reflected on the river and the air was full of sounds not from birds but from machines, I often sat by my window and thought of my ancestors. Did they ever imagine that one of their daughters would one day ride machines that flew across the ground, or speak in classrooms where knowledge from every corner of the earth was shared? Did they know that their stories of survival would carry me through sleepless nights of study, when I wanted to give up but remembered their courage? I like to believe that they walk with me, unseen, nodding when I take in new knowledge, smiling when I translate those lessons into visions for home.

Studying in China reshaped me not by changing my skin or my tongue, but by expanding the horizons of my mind. I learned to question not just what is, but what could be. I learned that culture is not a prison, but a root — it grounds you, but it does not have to confine you.

I can still wear my traditional dress, still paint my face in the colours of Huli, still dance when the kundu drum calls, but now I also know how to navigate a city of millions, how to read the signs of technology, how to write visions for development that might one day lift the children of my valley into new possibilities. I am not less Huli because I lived in China; I am more. I am stretched, layered, opened.

And yet, this expansion also comes with pain. To walk between worlds is to know longing — longing for the simplicity of home when you are abroad, and longing for the possibilities of abroad when you are home. I have come to accept that I will always carry this tension, like two rivers flowing within me, never fully merging, never fully apart. Perhaps this is the true meaning of growth — not to find a final resting place, but to learn to live with the flow of contradictions.

The most inward lesson I carry from China is about time. In Hela, time feels slow, measured by sun and season, by the ripening of fruit, by the rhythm of ceremonies. In China, time raced. Cities changed in a year, technologies upgraded in months, entire neighborhoods rebuilt in weeks. At first, I resisted, I longed for the slow pace of the mountains. But then I realised something: both speeds are needed. Too much speed, and you forget the meaning of roots. Too much slowness, and you risk being left behind by the world. I learned that I must become a woman of both times — to carry the patience of the garden and the urgency of the city within me.

And so as I close this chapter of my life, I find myself not asking "Who am I now?" but rather, "Who am I becoming?" Identity, I realise, is not a destination but a bridge. I am a bridge between PNG and China, between mist and neon, between kundu drums and digital screens. To be such a bridge is not always easy; sometimes it feels like being stretched too thin, like carrying the weight of two worlds. But it is also a gift, because a bridge connects. And perhaps my life's purpose is not simply to live on one side or the other, but to hold open the possibility of crossing, for myself and for others.

I think of the children in Hela, walking barefoot on the cold earth, eyes wide with questions about a world they have not yet seen. I think of the young students in China, racing on e-bikes, their lives already entangled with technologies that seem like magic to us. Both sets of children deserve to dream, to walk into a future where their potential is not crushed by lack or by ignorance. My journey has convinced me that such a future is possible — but only if we learn from one another, only if we are brave enough to cross the bridges of culture and knowledge.

What, then, is the meaning of my years in China? It is not simply that I earned degrees or that I saw wonders of technology.

It is that I learned how porous the self can be, how open the future is, how deeply connected humanity becomes when we dare to look beyond borders. I am leaving with more questions than answers, but perhaps that is the gift. For questions are seeds, and seeds grow into visions, and visions into change.

So here I stand, between worlds. The mist of Hela still clings to me, and the lights of Wuhan still glow in my memory. I am no longer only the girl who left her mountains, nor only the woman who studied in foreign cities. I am something in between, something still forming. And maybe that is enough.

As I take my final steps on this journey, I whisper to myself the same words I wrote in my notebook under a tree at BLCU, when it all began: "This is only the beginning." The bridge is built, the path is open, and I will keep walking — carrying both worlds in my heart, carrying both past and future in my spirit, carrying the hope that one life lived between worlds can become a light for many others.

The End

GLOSSARY

- **Kaukau** - sweet potato

- **Bilum** - traditional woven string bag from PNG

- **Bilas** - decorations or traditional attire

- **Buai** - the betel nut that people chew, often mixed with lime and mustard.

- **Singsing** - traditional song and dance celebration in PNG

- **Mumu** - traditional Papua New Guinean earth oven

- **Yu orait?** - You alright?/Are you okay?

- **Em orait, yu save mi** - It's okay, you understand me.

- **Sista, helpim mi liklik** - Sister, help me a little.

- **Kundu** - traditional hand drum of PNG, used in music, dance and ceremonies.

- **Kunai grass** - tall, tough grass that grows in the highlands of PNG.

- **Ni hao** - hello

- **Ni chi ma?** - Are you eating?/Do you want to eat?

ABOUT THE AUTHOR

Betty Wakia was born in Madang, Papua New Guinea, and has spent much of her life studying and living abroad. She holds a Bachelor of Education from Tianjin University of Technology and Education (China), a Master's degree in Education from the University of South Wales (United Kingdom), and is currently pursuing a PhD in Ideological and Political Education at Wuhan University of Technology (China).

Her journey across cultures has shaped her perspective on resilience, identity, and belonging. Journey Between Worlds is her debut memoir, offering readers a rare and heartfelt glimpse into the connections between Papua New Guinea and China.

CAPTIONS OF PHOTOGRAPHS

Chapter 2: Betty and her father

Chapter 3: Betty, pictured in the front row, received the prestigious Chinese Government Scholarship (CSC) award in 2011 — featured in Post Courier Newspaper.

Chapter 5: Betty standing before the historic Forbidden City in Beijing

Chapter 11: Betty's graduation at Tianjin University of Technology and Education

Chapter 16: Betty proudly raising the PNG flag on the Great Wall of China

Chapter 18: Betty's first ride on the skytrain in Wuhan, Hubei Province